PORTRAIT OF THE BLUES

PORTRAIT OF THE BLUES

PAUL TRYNKA

PHOTOGRAPHS BY VAL WILMER

DA CAPO PRESS • New York

Editor: **Mike Evans**
Assistant Editor: **Humaira Husain**
Production Controller: **Candida Lane**
Picture Research: **Liz Fowler**
Art Editor: **Valerie Hawthorn**

Book Design: **David Palmer Design Practice**

First published in the United States of America in
1997 by Da Capo Press, Inc.
A Subsidiary of Plenum Publishing Corporation
233 Spring Street, New York, N.Y. 10013

First published in 1996 by Hamlyn in the
United Kingdom, an imprint of Reed Consumer
Books Limited, Michelin House, 81 Fulham Road,
London SW3 6RB

Copyright © 1996
Reed International Books Limited

ISBN 0-360-80779-3

Printed and bound in Hong Kong

CONTENTS

John Lee Hooker

FOREWORD

The Blues is life, it's as simple as that. It's been around since the world was born. I think the Blues started back in the Garden of Eden – when Adam and Eve got thrown out. Presidents, rich people, poor people; they can all relate to the Blues. There's something big about it, a deep feeling they can all relate to. The Blues is misery if you want misery. Happiness if you want happiness.

When I started out I never dreamed this music would get to be so big. I played the music I learned from my step-father, and I thought I was just a local boy, playing for local people. Then my first single, Boogie Chillen, hit like an earthquake! Later on when I got over to Europe I couldn't believe how they loved my music over there – they ate the Blues up like chocolate cake. People like The Rolling Stones, Eric Clapton, Van Morrison were into what I was doing, and I'm real proud of that. The music we play, me, BB King, people like that, that music is the roots. Rock music, everything else, is like a branch on the same tree. It all comes from the Blues. They dress it up a little, but it's the same thing.

A few years ago I said I wasn't going to make records any more; most of the record companies I'd been with were like a sack of snakes – they got rich quick, and I got poor quick. But my manager talked me into doing another one, and I found that young people were getting into my music again. They wanted the real stuff. That made me feel really good.

It's good that the kids listen to rock music, but they need to find out where it comes from, to find out about its roots. That's why I want young people to find out about Blues music, to discover the real, deep Blues. Because other forms of music, they might come, and they might go, but the Blues will still be here. Lots of the people, friends of mine, who played the real Blues, Muddy Waters, Albert King, Stevie Ray Vaughan, they've all gone. But their music is still here. The Blues will never die. Long as the world is going, the Blues will be here.

John Lee Hooker

Danny McLean

Paul Trynka

Val Wilmer with guitarist Willie Johnson, 1972

Paul Trynka

The author would like to acknowledge the invaluable help of many individuals. In particular I'd like to thank Gary Edwards, Michael Frank, Larry Garner, Steve Lee, Tina Mayfield, Kathleen McCreedy and Robert Stroger for their hospitality, Linda Hancock and Aisha Khan for their invaluable assistance with the transcripts, Neil Slaven for his suggestions and comments on the original manuscript, and Mike Evans, an editor to be treasured. This book would never have been completed without the assistance of Kathy Adam, Jeff Alperin, Gwyn Ashley, Jim Bateman, Rick Bates, Steve Beggs, Michael Blakemore, Dick Boak, Sam Burckhardt, Patrice Campbell, John Crosby, Patrick Day, Philip Dodd, Scott and Susan Duncan, Gary Hood, Kathleen Finigan, Mindy Giles, Bill Greensmith, Tom Heimdal, Claire Horton, Cilla Huggins, Mirek Juroslaw, Bruce Iglauer, Matthew Johnson, Cliff Jones, Mike Kappus, Danny and Jay Kessler, Edward Komera, Randy Labbe, Michael Leonard, David Less, Mark Lipkin, Annie Lockwood, Andy McKaie, Tom Nolan, Vaughan Oliver, Hugh Overton, Jerry Pillow, Lois Powell, Tom Radai, Sally Reeves, Fred Reif, Jack Rich, Samantha Richards, Alan Robinson, Jane Rose, Marty Salzman, Trevor Simpson, John Sinclair, Mark Skyer, Joel Slotnikoff, Kat Stratton, Bee Sumlin, Stackhouse Record Mart, Bernice Turner, and Richard Wootton. Although space unfortunately precludes me from mentioning the many books and other reference works consulted, particular thanks must go to Living Blues Magazine and the University of Mississippi for the use of their archives. And a very special thanks to all the interviewees for giving me their time and attention.

INTRODUCTION

The Blues is quite possibly the most visceral, emotionally charged art form we will ever know. Strange, then, that discussion of the subject is so often straitjacketed by reverence and intellectualisation. There seems a kind of cultural apartheid applied to Blues music, which tends to cause it to be either dismissed, or wrapped in a kind of airless academic cocoon. But Blues music isn't something that's distinct from Rock or other forms of modern popular music - it's simply Rock music in its primal, most vital state, before the attentions of marketing departments or name producers made Rock music just another product. It is no coincidence that Elvis Presley, in terms of commercial success the first white man to sing the Blues, was also the first Rock music product to be consciously marketed.

The development of Blues music anticipated, in countless ways, the development of Rock music. Convention has it that Cream or Led Zeppelin took Sixties Rock music to new heights of sophistication and musical extravagance, but even cursory study reveals that Otis Rush or Willie Dixon had explored the same territory 10 years before. During the months and years I spent tracking down and talking to the 60 musicians interviewed in this book, I realised that their personal stories, too, both anticipated and exceeded most of the tales of deprivation or excess that emerged from the Sixties. At the time when most of them were making music, there was no blueprint for its construction, no maps for the territory they were exploring. Although their attitudes and themes vary hugely, from bitter tales of exploitation to inspiring accounts of transcendent creativity, there is a consistent freshness about these stories, free from the constraints of public relations, or a need to impress. Although many of these interviewees were in their seventies, or older, and although several of them are no longer with us, they will remain, for me, forever young. Popular music is distinguished, perhaps even defined, by its ephemeral nature, by the impetus for constant change. Yet the achievements of these pioneers, whose presence is as tangible in the music of Primal Scream or Portishead as in Blues Rock, constitute a vital foundation for the music that followed. It makes all of popular music more substantial, gives it an added gravitas, and a sense of history.

When Val Wilmer and I discussed this book, we decided to make its images, both verbal and photographic, as honest and unfiltered as possible. We had a common urge to go to the source of these stories, to be told in musicians' own words. We wanted to document the diversity of voices and moods which is often obscured by observers' preconceptions. Some of these images, therefore, are the stuff of popular legend: dusty porches, parched cottonfields and casual racism. But these images are only part of a bigger picture, which takes in the humour, sophistication, inspiration and aspirations of all of these diverse characters. To postulate a definitive, causal theory of the evolution of the Blues would be to diminish this music, to put it in a box and imprison it. These diverse first-hand tales and images make up a bigger story, of the music that forms the wellspring for so many of the attitudes and the sounds of the Twentieth Century. It's the story of a profound cultural movement. It's also the story of some of the best damn pop music ever made.

ROOTS

I'm on the porch of Jack Owens' shack in Bentonia, Mississippi, listening as the now-frail singer picks up his cheap Eko guitar and starts singing about the devil. Anyone who's ever seen a Budweiser or Heineken advertisement would recognise the surroundings, which look like a film set filled with clichéd props: rusty Oldsmobile, Gilby's gin bottle and a howling dog named Boy, sniffing around the yard. But as we empty the gin, and Owens sings his eerily haunting lines, answering each one with a phrase from his minor-tuned guitar, a connection suddenly becomes clear: this is Africa talking to me.

Brewton Alabama 1973

Jack Owens with his late wife Mabel, Bentonia Mississippi 1972

Most of the elements of Owens' playing are familiar, but in this context both his phrasing and tonality seem deeply unAmerican, eerily reminiscent of Rouicha Mohamed, a Moroccan lute player I'd heard over a bowl of kif one balmy night in Tangiers. Even though the African roots of the Blues have been well documented, the similarities between Owens' and Mohamed's minor mode lines and elongated verses were startling. Yet although the connection seemed overwhelmingly obvious, the mechanism behind it was almost unfathomable.

The process behind the evolution of the Blues has exercised musicologists for a number of decades now, for although it's possible to say where the music came from, it's not so easy to say how it came about. We can cite the African influences in the music, and its relationship to spirituals and work songs. Yet even WC Handy, an educated black musician who would later become known as The Father Of The Blues, was staggered by how alien this new music seemed when he encountered a loose-limbed musician singing a mournful song about the Southern Railroad in Tutwiler Mississippi, 1903. Handy would later rationalise the music he'd heard and help popularise the idiom. Ma Rainey, too, who became one of the first great female Blues singers, encountered the music by chance in 1902. Handy and Rainey both found familiar elements in the early Blues they heard, but were still stunned by its alien impact. We will never know whether the musicians they both heard were undistinguished exponents of a fairly common format, or whether they'd both chanced on unique, uncredited architects of the new music – there are those who believe that Handy's unknown musician was Charley Patton, one of the very first documented Blues singers. What is certain is that the Blues did not evolve purely as a result of geographical and sociological forces: as with any musical movement, from the British Invasion to the Seattle Scene, the environment may have helped shape the music, but was not responsible for it. It's people, and not places, that make music, and there are doubtless many individual architects of the early Blues whose names will remain unknown forever.

But of any environment which nurtured an art form, the Mississippi Delta stands alone. Although other areas in the United States, most notably Texas, would exert an important influence, American Blues are firmly rooted in the soil of the Delta, the centre of cotton farming and the sharecropping system established after the Civil War. Before the Second World War around three-quarters of the African American population lived in the rural South – and the sharecropping system was the most significant form of employment. The sharecropping system was established for assertedly philanthropic reasons following the Reconstruction: a sharecropper would be allotted a plot of land, would tend the cotton, and split the value of the crop with the plantation owner; the price of seeds, tools, and whatever advances made for living expenses would be deducted from his share. Many of the plantation owners could not resist the opportunity to swindle the sharecroppers at the year-end settle, condemning them to a precarious existence which involved sinking deeper into debt or starting up elsewhere.

In the social system exemplified by sharecropping, music took on a new significance as a rare outlet for free expression, communication and celebration. By the end of the century, a rich and wide black musical tradition had become established through most of the Delta – spirituals, work songs and field hollers, string bands, and fife and drum bands. At the same time, black musicians became acquainted

Meridian Mississippi, 1974

13

with European folk and embryonic American hillbilly traditions. By 1894, guitars
became available through the Sears Roebuck, and later Montgomery Ward mail
order catalogues. Cheap, portable and versatile, the guitar would eventually become
the Delta's most popular instrument. Some of the stylistic devices used by the early
black guitarists, alternating bass patterns on the lower strings with chords on the
treble strings, were undoubtedly European, but other distinctly African techniques
evolved, most notably that of playing the guitar with a slider, penknife or bottleneck. To this day, a Delta tradition still exists of making a rudimentary one-string
guitar or 'diddley bow', played with a slider, which is essentially identical to African
single string bows such as the Bentwa. The diddley bow slider, used with a guitar,
rendered the European 12-tone scale obsolete, and bent or flattened notes, already
a part of the singing vocabulary, became part of the instrumental vocabulary, too.
When WC Handy saw his mysterious musician playing slide guitar using a knife in

Sunday morning, Bentonia Mississippi 1973

Fifth Street, Meridian Mississippi 1974

1903, the technique was brand new. Over the next 20 years or so it would become hugely popular, and the Blues would become well established.

The move from old fashioned folk ballads such as 'John Henry', or jump up songs, to what we now recognise as the Blues was a gradual one. The dividing line between Gospel and Blues could be narrow, turning on subject matter or choice of venues: for instance, Blind Willie Johnson, a hell-fire gospel preacher and singer – as well as versatile bottleneck guitarist – had a profound influence on many Blues players, including Fred McDowell. What we now think of as the archetypal Blues form, the 12-bar, which appeared as early as 1900 with songs such as 'Joe Turner', would not be regarded as definitive until the Twenties, when the commercial possibilities of 'The Blues' were first grasped, and hundreds of those forgettable 12-bar songs were marketed as sheet music. Before that point Blues numbers were just as likely to be heard in an 8-bar format.

Whatever the niceties of defining when the music fully evolved, the Blues had a dramatic impact. Just as Rock music would give voice to a whole new generation in the Sixties, Blues expressed the aspirations and complaints of the 20th-century African American. It would prove a potent vehicle for their concerns.

William Ferris / Centre for Southern Folklore Archive

Ebet Roberts / Redferns

15

Napoleon Strickland playing one string guitar, Senatobia Mississippi 1970

Cedell Davis

Cedell Davis:

Me and Isaiah Ross, Dr Ross, grew up together over there, used to play together – lived about three blocks apart [1]. I went there one Sunday and they had one of these diddley bows upside the house, on the outside. Well, it sounded good to me – I ain't never saw nothing like that before. I went home and made me one. From that, that started me wanting to play the guitar.

What a diddley bow is, there's one string of wire – way back then, when you buy a broom they had a special kind of wire was wrapped around the bottom to hold the straw on the broom. That's the kind of wire we would use, because it was smaller than hay-baling wire – it sound better. And I learned how to play the thing. You'd nail it up against a wall. You got one nail here, you wrapped the wire around it real tight, twist it so it won't come loose, then you drive it into the wall, tight as you can get it. Pull the wire stretched tight as you can, do the same thing at the other end. OK, one up there, one down here. You get you a glass snuff bottle and put that in between the string and the wall, and press it down and that what gets you the sound [2]. Then you find you a cake flavour bottle and that's what you pick it with, slide it up and down and it changes the tuning, similar to the violin. The diddley bow goes

16

Eugene Powell, 1976

way back. It comes from Africa. I got one now that I made, it's in the Little Rock Museum there, been in there for over 10 years.

Eugene Powell:

I don't know nothing, but something they call the Blues. Now Blues been around a long time. I was born in 1908, and it was out far back as I remember when I was a little boy, folks were playing violin, some people call it a fiddle, a guitar, and some of them that old Jew's harp thing, and some had a French harp. Now there always was some music around, but white people played popular music – that's what they played all the time. Coloured people, he lit out trying to play the Blues, playing about some woman that he like and singing about her, trying to draw her attention. So I would say that's the way that was.

I played and tried to sing when I was just a little boy. My mama bought me a guitar from Sears, Roebuck. I don't know if she paid two and a half, maybe three dollars. I couldn't sing nothing! They had an old piece long time ago when I was a boy about Boll Weevil [3]. This is how it came about. Used to be years ago, my mama and them said, they used to raise cotton and corn in the South. But they got to places way out in the hills where they was farming down there in Jackson, and it got to where they couldn't raise nothing 'cause of them things they called the Boll Weevil. The Weevils got so thick, they eat up the crops. Well then they had to quit doing that, and they changed from that to raising fruits, and stuff like in the garden, they start to raising orange and apple trees, water melon patches, and well, they be playing there, singing all that kind of stuff. And that old Boll Weevil song it come out. I can remember the old folk singing it. And the old blind fella made that song about the Boll Weevil – he sang, 'Boll Weevil went to Memphis, take Christmas in, he come back singing this song, I'm back again.' I heard that from an old blind man who used to come to our house. It might seem funny to you, but it's not funny to me 'cause I know, but there have been some blind people could play the guitar better than people that could see.

The Blues come from people out in the fields, working and going on. You sing about . . . most people sings about a woman, about a girl, about hard times, and all stuff like that. When I started out I was playing with a fella called Johnny Holst. But after they heard me play they always said I was better than Johnny. I liked that, I want to beat somebody doing something, you know how a child is. I'd make music up of my own. The Blues is a thing that you can make up like you want to – but try and make it up right, make everything correspond. And good. Then the folks'll like it. Most Blues, you be singing about some woman, a girl or sump'n. About some girlfriend you like, she's trying to put you down for another boy, you got to make up, I used to love you but you shouldn't treat me like that, stuff like that! Another one I used to play was Hesitating Blues – you didn't (ever) hear that, did you [4]? I done forgotten now how to sing it. And I made up my own. I used to try and play like everybody, but I quit and played in my own way.

Yank Rachell:

I traded my mandolin for a pig. Well, I was about 12 years old and my father was a farmer way out in the country, wasn't no concrete then nowhere . . . so I was in the country, a little old boy going down a dusty road, and there was a man sitting on a porch playing a mandolin, a mandolin with a stripe on the back – a round back. So the man sitting on the porch, I went by there, and said, Mr Hawkins, what is that you got? He said, a mandolin, son. I said, uh I like that, let me see it. I hit a lick or two on it – I couldn't play nothing then, I was just a little boy. He said, let me sell it to you. Said, I ain't got no money, Mr Hawkins . . . what you take for it? He said five dollars, I said, uh . . . I got a pig I'll trade you for it. My mother gave me a pig you know, we were in the country, we raised a lot of hogs, and my mother gave me a pretty little black fine blood hog. I said alright suh, I went back home, where my father raised plenty corn, I called the little pig out, got a tow sack so I could put him in there, and carried him on round to the man's house, right round the picket, I didn't let my mother see. So I went round and said, I got the pig, and he said, oh yeah, take the mandolin. Which ain't no value to what the hog would be when he grew up, you know, but I didn't know and didn't care!

I got the mandolin, and I come on home with it, couldn't play anything on it, but kept on hitting them eight strings. My father would say, boy put that thing down, I got to go to work in the morning – I say alright suh and I put it down, he go to bed, and when he get up and go to work I get up and get it again.

My mother she didn't say nothing for a while, she went on. Later on she got up one morning, and sat by the fire, she said, James, I said Mama, she said where your pig? I ain't seen that pig in a day or two. I say, I ain't either, Mama. I know where the pig was, but I say I ain't. She said well, see can you find that pig, I said yes Mama, I got up, went to the barn and stood there about 10 minutes, I didn't stay long enough, I come back. You see that pig? Mama I ain't seen that pig nowhere. She said, well where you go? I said I went all around the picket, everywhere, she said, you lying – you better find that pig. She said what is that thing you playing? A mandolin. Where you get it from? I said I got it from a fella down the street, down the road there. He give it to you? I said, no Mama, he didn't give it to me, that man. She said you didn't steal it did you? See them days and time when I come up, 60 years ago, if you steal something the old folk beat you to death. I said no Mama. Where you get it from? I said oh Mama, I got it. She didn't say nothing, but she went out in the yard, to the tree out there full of switches, she got every switch off that tree, the tree willow, had all them long switches. She come in there. You gonna tell me where you got that thing? I wouldn't tell her then. Pull your clothes off! She said, I ain't gonna whup them clothes – I bought them, so ain't no way I'm gonna whup 'em. I'm gonna whup your meat. Pull them clothes off, boy. I come in and cried. I told her, Mama, I traded the pig for it. She said I ought to whup you to death, we were gonna eat the meat, now how we gonna eat that thing? That's what she told me about the mandolin. Then she went on.

Honeyboy Edwards:

What I think about it, and what I get into it, I think the Blues come from slavery time. Back in slave times, people and convicts and prison songs and things like that. They would sing, holler songs in the fields to make the day longer, if they working and singing, they had to get it off their mind if they was gonna make the day. And the Blues in the Twenties, like Blind Lemon, Texas Alexander and all those other guys that recorded, they were just playing the same songs but they changed it over to the Blues – they said this is the Blues. And it was the Blues. Then up in the Thirties and Forties they got the Maudlin Blues. So the Blues come from way back but it sprung, the main thing come from slavery time, holler songs in the fields and things like that, they didn't know nothing to do but sing, and they called it the Blues. And them songs would make them go on, make an easier day by them singing and going on (sings).

James 'Son' Thomas, Leland Mississippi 1978

My father showed me my chords and things. He had played violin and guitar, he had quit playing, but he was interested in me playing. When we was down South, the people had bands, string bands, they didn't have no tuners then, they'd tune to their sounds and they wasn't that much off. My father, I don't know where he started up, he was playing in 1920, then I don't know why, but he slowed up playing. He still liked to always take the guitar and play it, but he didn't play dances or nothing.

At the time my father was playing, there was a few Blues, but not too many. My dad would play things like 'John Henry Was A Steel Driving Man' [5]. And sort of like Ragtime music. And 'Stackolee'. My daddy used to play that well before Lloyd Price made a hit with it. 'Bring it On Home To My House Baby, Ain't Nobody Home With Me' – that's the kind of stuff he played. Before Blind Lemon came out playing the Blues, before then it was a whole lot of ragtime stuff. When Blind Lemon came out playing the Blues, that started putting something on the players' minds – so they started playing a different type, a new style of blues. Blind Lemon, he had a whole lot of flying chords, attractive chords, he played in A, and then he had no turnaround – he played everything straight through, but we have a turnaround now. We turn around and go again, but Blind Lemon he played straight through on one chord.

Othar Turner (drum) and Napoleon Strickland (fife), Gravel Springs Mississippi 1970

The Blues works in different ways. If you play it good enough it makes people lonesome, sad. But it can be about having a good time. Blues is more than the one thing, it's a mind thing, when you learn it and get used to it. It's an attractive thing to your mind.

Jr Kimbrough:

When I was young, we would work all week long and play on weekend. It was quiet in the week – now you get these youngsters started running all ways, but then everything was quiet all through the week. An acoustic guitar now, you can't hardly hear from here to the corn yard. Back in them days you could hear an acoustic guitar a long way – that's on account of the elements, there's too many machines running now, drowning the sound down, if you don't have an electric guitar now you can hardly hear nothing, but back in them days you could hear an acoustic guitar way across town over there.

Back then lots of them was farming, and some was working what we call public work [6]. Picking cotton at two and a half a hundred – what you call sharecropping. It wasn't no machines then, nothing but mules, plying mules, picking cotton by hand [7]. Then share-cropping, you would split the money from the cotton less your expenses, but that was a hard way of making a living. They was more jobs for people then, but they wasn't paying people as much as they is paying them now. A lot of them older people would work for 50 cents a day.

Eddie Kirkland:

My mama ended up in South West Alabama, a place called Dothan, and the only work you could get back then was picking cotton, working in the fields – it would be 50, 60,

70 people in the field picking cotton. That's where I first heard the Blues, and spiritual music. Early in the morning, they would sing spirituals – then when the sun gets hot, round 110 degrees in the afternoon, that's when they start singing the Blues, to help them get through the day. And them songs accumulated in my ear 'cause my mother had to take me to the cotton fields when I was two years old, and sit me on the end of the cotton row. That's where I started getting the Blues feeling in me.

Homesick James:

The Blues was in Europe before it even came here. Ever since there's been a world there' been the Blues. Don't let nobody tell you it come from field hollers – rich guys got the Blues, like the president got the Blues right now. Know what I'm saying? The Blues ain't what people call it. Blues ain't no hard times. Blues is when you got a problem you can't solve. That's what the Blues is. Baby crying and hollering, want his milk and can't get a bottle, he got the Blues. That's what time it is. And don't let nobody tell you that.

Jessie Mae Hemphill:

My granddaddy's music, it come from Africa [8]. My granddaddy knowed it, and his daddy knowed it too. Granddaddy used to play his drums everywhere – everybody would want him for a picnic, he couldn't get around all the picnics there was. He had a big old drum, he played the fice [9] himself, and a guy called Will Head would beat the drums, and Alec Askew would play the kithers, them two little drums.

Jessie Mae Hemphill at the Rust College Blues Festival, Holly Springs Mississippi 1988

22

Blues dance, Bentonia Mississippi 1976

Whenever I wanted anything my granddaddy would make it. He made me a drum, a bedroom suit(e), and a little old poster bed. He made money off that, everybody round here wanted him to make a poster bed. I was his eyes – he had cataracts grow in his eyes 'cause he was a blacksmith's boy – the blue light ruined his eyes. My first drum, my granddaddy made for me, about this big. He get him some tin, some of that light tin, and white folks here, when they killed cows and things round here they'd give him the hide, and then me and him would take it home, and put it on a bowl and stretch it, then we'd get some sandpaper and scrape it, get all the hair off it, I tell you he learned me how to do everything. And then we'd get ready to put it on the drum. He made the rims out of some hickory – we went out in the woods and found a hickory tree, I said granddaddy this looks like hickory, come here, he come and he would feel it, to tell if it was hickory or not, say yeah this is hickory, we'd take that, cut that bark off it, cut it, make the rim for the drum, put that rim across there, and put those screws across there, just like a real bought drum, you couldn't tell. I painted it green and you couldn't even tell it wasn't a drum you'd just bought. I sounded good with that cow head in there, man. I asked him to make me a fiddle, and he made me a fiddle, too.

My granddaddy would play all kinds of songs. 'My Carrie', 'Casey Jones', 'Alabama Bound' and 'Yellow Mama Blues' . . feel like jumping through the keyhole in your door! We'd laugh when he played that – I said, I know how you're feeling grandpa, feel like jumping through the keyhole in your door. Lord that would tickle everybody. All of the white folk were crazy about him and the children. He was friendly with everybody, but he would play more for white people round here. At their houses for them big dances, the rich white folk would get him to play, and all three of the girls and me, they would tell him, let them all come over there. They liked to do waltzes. Square dances. Granddaddy would call and they would do it. It looked so purty. I was two years old, and he played for a white lady down here, a rich woman, and it was in the summer time. The door was open and they was there dancing in the hall, and I was kidding Miss Logan how she was doing the time dance. Every time my granddaddy would say Bring Your Partners she'd swing and I'd swing

Skip James, Hammersmith Gaumont, London 1967

there out in the yard, she didn't see me, I was mocking her and she didn't know it! And I learned to swing dance too. He'd play some good songs, I liked that square dancing and that Tennessee Waltz, I was crazy about that myself, I just wasn't big enough to swing it out like I wanted! Ha ha ha!

Mr Hogmoore, Mr Snow and all of them was double rich white folks. They was nice rich folks, though. Let me tell you, all the rich people would come to that dance. One night they got to fighting, granddaddy say there's gonna be a fight, fastened the fiddle in the case and tipped out the back door and he cut out, him and Ted. They went to shooting, and one man in front of him ran into a telegraph pole. The telegraph pole knocked him back where he was and he said to the telegraph pole, excuse me mister! Then he ran round the other way. Ran into the post and knocked himself out almost. Saying to that post excuse me mister!

Pops Staples:

I didn't want to play the Blues, but when I grew up that was about the only thing you could hear. My daddy raised cotton, corn, peanuts and hay. We made a good living, I have never suffered 'cause my father was a very good provider. We didn't have much money but we always had plenty to eat.

Where I lived, Drew Mississippi, there was the Dockery Plantation, and there they had a couple called Dick and James, who just used to play on the street. Then on the weekend Charley Patton would play. He lived on my plantation. He was a good man far as I know, I didn't know his life and everything – I wasn't strong enough to go up to him. But I'd see him play at the fish fries. Maybe someone would have a big house, and they would cook chicken and chitlin' on a Saturday evening, and Saturday night they would have a dance. Ladies would be cooking in the kitchen, and there's a room over there where they're gambling, playing cards, and a big room out in front, that's where we'd play and dance. And that's how I got to be playing the Blues, 'cause we had so many houses, but didn't have enough guitar players to go round. So I'd slip over there and play – in those days, the parents didn't want their children to listen to blues, they said the guitar was the devil's music. My daddy didn't know.

Yank Rachell:

Me and my brother, we liked to play picnics – out in a grove, like a shade, trees and everything. You had lights – they put corn oil in a Coca Cola bottle: a Coca Cola bottle used to be little then, you put some rag in there and soak it, stick it down and make a light. They had the lights hanging all around there on a string, and we'd play at the picnic, and have a big time, man. Them girls dancing, dust fly all over. Then we'd play for country dances, call 'em fish fries. Like this time of year now, when I was in the country we'd be busy playing every Friday and Saturday night. Ladies be in the kitchen cooking fish, put a table 'cross the door, and they'd be in there cooking, you want a fish sandwich they'd give you a fish sandwich, then we'd be out there dancing, break the floor down dancing, some guy out there in the barn shooting crap and losing money, come back, his wife dancing with somebody, he start a big fight, go to shooting and some of them jumping out of the window. I run in and stayed with a mule one night, got so rough there. Old mule say 'whu' to me. I said 'whu' right back to him.

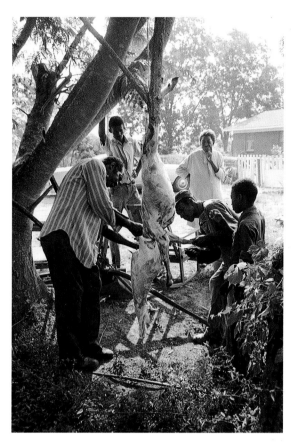

Skinning a goat, Bentonia Mississippi 1973

Othar Turner:

What we play, the fice and drums, it's a calling thing. When they give a picnic, they'd get up way early in the morning, take the drums right up over that hill, and play them. Then after a few hours people would be coming from miles around, it ended up you'd get so many folk turn up for the picnic they have to turn sideways to get through.

It started from Africa. That's what I was told when I was young and just started up. When anybody would cease, that would be the notifier. You'd get that fice and play them drums and march behind the casket all the way to the cemetery. After that it started playing at the parties, like your birth party. Family union, they invite me man, I'd play at them [10]. There they'd march, dance all round there, and there's some fun in it.

This cane I play ain't nothing but a fishing cane. But a cane, you can do more than just fishing with it. Now you can take this cane and split it and make chairs out of it, or make baskets out of it, make chair bottoms out of it if you know how. That's the way this fice is, it's just a straight cane. Got leaves on, you strip them off, strip them all down, cut it off smooth like I got it here. Now you can't make a fice out of one joint of cane, you understand that. Look, there's a joint here and a joint there. Now how can I blow a fice that short? I got to have some distance. You cannot bore a hole in a fice with a pocket knife. You got to get you a red hot iron and burn that first hole in the cane. Then you go back and make your holes there, and you get this cane here. But now that fice, it ain't gonna do nothing if you lay there and look at it, that's what a heap people can't see.

Honeyboy Edwards:

The way my daddy learned to play was by listening to old time people. On a lot of the numbers – they didn't really play the bottleneck blues like they did later, they'd play slide but they'd play it John Henry style. It was mostly slow slide. They had this old style of playing, but it worked all right.

But my daddy had a rough life and his time, that he told me, he used to give country dances too. Stayed on a white man's place one time, he told me, and this man was over to his dance messing with the black people and this guy came over and killed him – shot the man off his horse. They were miserable days back then. When I met Big Joe, and he came with me and said, can I take Honey out to Greenville, I'll take care of him, my daddy said, Honey can go if he wants, I don't care [11]. There ain't nothing to do on the farm, there ain't no work out there – he can go. I don't care.

Chapter I - **Notes**

1   Over there: Tunica, Mississippi

2   ie acts as a bridge, and together with the building to which it is attached, as a soundbox

3   'Boll Weevil', a folk ballad popular during World War One, and was later recorded by Leadbelly. Powell cannot remember the name of the guitarist who introduced the song to him

4   'Hesitation Blues', or 'Hesitating Blues', was an early Blues song, widely recorded in the Twenties

5   'John Henry' and 'Stackolee' are two of the most celebrated early black folk ballads, predating what we'd regard as Blues songs

6   Public work: domestic service in white households

7   Hundred: hundredweight. Plying: ploughing

8   Sid Hemphill, Jessie Mae's grandfather, was one of the most celebrated exponents of Mississippi fife and drum music. See Chapter Seven of *The Land Where The Blues Began* by Alan Lomax

9   Fice: fife

10   Union: Reunion

11   Edwards went on the road with Big Joe Williams in 1932

James Davis, Henderson Georgia 1978

RAMBLING ON MY MIND

Robert Jr Lockwood, the legendary guitarist who was taught by Robert Johnson, is a mysterious and elusive figure. Standing outside a small motel in Helena, Arkansas, the culmination of months of phonecalls and letters, I find out just how elusive. He tells me I don't exist. The meeting we'd arranged didn't exist, the letters I had written hadn't arrived . . . as far as Lockwood and family are concerned, they've never heard of me.

The friend I've brought along for the meeting is now on the verge of losing her temper. She's a seasoned music promoter, but her protestations to Annie Lockwood – 'he's a good guy' – are met only with a withering laugh and a look that speaks volumes. Reflecting on the implication that I'm both a figment of my own imagination, and an asshole, I decide that now might be a good time to leave.

Banjo playing composer Gus Cannon at home, Memphis 1971.

It was three months later, seven hundred miles away, when I finally tracked Lockwood down. Not a word was mentioned about our earlier meeting, nor any clue as to why he'd now agreed to see me. But the ritual I'd been forced through somehow made it even more moving to be sitting opposite this dignified figure, who had first hit the road 60 years ago. Lockwood is an avuncular, almost regal man, laid back as he describes some of the experiences of his solitary rambling years. The most common adjective he uses is 'strange'. Or 'peculiar', an appropriate word for a life defined by chance encounters, and bizarre experiences. Such as being locked up under the vagrancy law, purely to entertain your jailers and their friends. Or to go looking for Robert Johnson, only to find the man you are searching for is in fact yourself. Or to find that history credits Elvis Presley, rather than Louis Jordan, with the creation of Rock'n'Roll.

Just as I'm surmising that Lockwood's calmness is a reaction to the unpredictability of his life, he tells me about seeing off record company exploitation by telling one executive 'I'll blow your motherfucking head off,' concluding the anecdote with a smile. Then I remember why I didn't argue when I was told I didn't exist. Because parts of Lockwood's life will always remain a mystery, and we will never fully understand his experiences, or the strategies he used to cope with them. Our stereotyped visions of the wandering hobo, or of the live fast die young Bluesmen who made pacts with the Devil, are too simplistic for such men. Lockwood and his like are complex personalities, who exist outside media clichés, capable of creative genius but forced at times to contemplate thuggery merely to survive. And Lockwood, of course, is one of hundreds of Blues singers who hobo'd through the American South before the Second World War, following in the footsteps of WC Handy's mysterious guitar player. So often neatly characterised later as being part of a genre, these early players were as diverse as they come.

Many early Delta Blues players cite Charley Patton as the first influential guitarist they can remember; in turn, Patton is thought to have been taught guitar by Henry Sloan, who lived on the same Dockery Plantation. Although Patton's first records were made at the end of the decade, his reputation spread through Mississippi throughout the Twenties, and he would prove a profound influence on the likes of Son House, Robert Johnson, Howlin' Wolf and even Muddy Waters.

Patton emerged during a uniquely productive period in American musical history. It's likely that the First World War played a part in fostering cross fertilisation of the various Blues styles, as players from different regions exchanged ideas overseas or in military camps – certainly, even before record labels such as OKeh and Paramount latched onto the Blues in the Twenties, Patton and his contemporaries were building up audiences at picnics, fish fries, juke joints, and on the street. Many singers travelled widely: Blind Lemon Jefferson, who would almost single-handedly found a whole Texas Blues tradition, is thought to have travelled through Mississippi, Oklahoma and the Carolinas, as well as his native state. There were players, such as Lonnie Johnson, from New Orleans, who emerged from an urban background, but in the main it was the rural singers such as Patton, Jefferson, and Texas Alexander who firmly established the music in the American South. They did it the hard way.

Son House, Hammersmith Gaumont, London 1967

Guitar Shorty and Willie Johnson, Elm City North Carolina 1972

Yank Rachell:

I used to hobo with a suitcase and a mandolin. Throw 'em on there and catch the next one, get on that boxcar and ride. One guy tried to make me jump off the car one night, I wouldn't, he come over there, it was cold, he come on top, we was in an open car, told us to get off, said I ain't getting off man, he said I bet you will, I said I bet I won't . . . We had a pistol, me and John, an old pistol with us [1]. Then he decided he didn't want to bother us. Yeah, we'd hobo all the time, go somewhere, buy some popcorn, crackers, candy and eat it, going on about our business, we didn't care. We'd sleep different places. If it was warm we wouldn't sleep. Go out there and lay down somewhere. One night when I was laying down this old guy come and try to take my shoes, a hobo – took my shoes. Yeah, me and Sleepy John went through some.

When it was cold we'd go to somebody's house, we didn't care who they was, we'd go up and knock and tell them we had music – y'all play music, come on in, play me a piece. We'd go in and play and sometimes stay two, three days – they glad to have us. Wouldn't charge us or nothing. Then in the summer we'd leave home about 12 o'clock at night and go to people's houses, go to their door and go to playing music. And some of them would come out, they was so glad, they enjoyed it, some be upstairs and partying and drop money down, one boy blowed a jug and he had so much money in the jug one night he couldn't blow it, they'd filled it up with dimes and quarters, hee hee hee. Nickels and pennies and things.

Homesick James:

I'm a drifter and I'm a loner. I stay by myself – I don't put up with no yak, from womens that blab blab blab. I don't put up with no bullshit, I ain't gonna have it. I'm a loner and I drift around. I been through every county in the US, literally every state. I would get around by train, bus. Wasn't no money in them days, but I'd get enough for my bus fare, nickel here, dime there, and I'm goin' and goin' and gone. I likes to get around, don't like to stay in one place long.

Wasn't like it is now, everybody killing each other. Back then if people could do something to help you they would help you. I didn't have to worry about going in no strange place, I didn't know where I'd be staying but there'd always be someone to say come on over to my house. Musicians, they ain't no problem. I played with Blind Boy Fuller in North Carolina, I start playing, people say there's this young kid down there, then they'd come and turn up [2]. It was a lot of fun in those days. Now it ain't no fun, it's just work. I had a better time then than I have now. I didn't never have no hard times. I'm having a harder time now.

Honeyboy Edwards:

Some places it was pretty rough. It was some good people and some bad people everywhere. It was some white people down there [3] at the time was mean, and I played for a lot of white dances down there and they treated me real nice, they'd bring me back home in the car, pay me what they said they was gonna pay me, give me my drinks and my meal free. But sometimes a musician caught it pretty bad 'cause most of the farmers figure if you played music you wouldn't work on the farm. And they needed people to work on the cotton and corn. And (if) a musician make a little money on a Friday and Saturday night he wouldn't go out there in the field working, he'd stay sleeping all day long where they couldn't see him. At night he'd come out. They see you with a guitar some of them would be thinking, he ain't gonna work. Then in the Forties it changed a whole lot where they didn't need nobody working in the fields 'cause they've got mechanicals – machines to pick the cotton [4].

Every once in a while you'd get arrested for vagrancy. They used to have in Greenwood what they call a hobo law, if you're out after nine o'clock at night, like curfew hours. Then they had another thing, like vagrancy. If they catch you walking in the streets they could arrest you, make you stay in jail two or three days for vagrancy. They'd do that just once a year in the summer, when the farmer needed people real bad. But I wasn't bothered too much 'cause I had a girlfriend working for the white peoples, in service, a big house, she went to work in the morning about seven or eight o'clock and I be back there in bed sleeping. Listening to the old radio. And when she get off work around one or two o'clock we'd take a bath and walk downtown and go to the picture show. I always know how to get around, I wasn't bothered too much.

When I was travelling around going from different cities, if I was going from Greenwood to Memphis I'd catch the freight train – I'd hobo. Sometime if I get up to Tennessee, and I go somewhere short I'd catch me a ride then. Most of the people then was crazy about guitar players and if they be riding they stop and pick you up. Didn't have to worry about no rides. But if I'm going a long way, Memphis to St Louis, I'd catch a freight. Get off in the yard, hang till the freight train gets quiet, then I walk down the street and catch the city bus going downtown. They would put you in the county farm if they catch you some-time. That's something like a little county penitentiary, it wasn't the state penitentiary. In Texas they would make you pick peas, in Mississippi they would make you chop cotton if they catch you.

I got caught one time. I wasn't but 16 then and didn't know no better. But they didn't work me so hard 'cause I was so young, so I tote water, carried water to the prison, I wasn't doing nothing. But after I found that out I (was) never caught no more, 'cause when I'd catch a freight train it would be up in the yard, and when the train slows down I gets off. They have to catch you on the train – if they don't catch you on there they don't know where you come from, but if they catch you up there they got proof. So I get off before anybody see me, duck out in the woods for maybe eight or 10 minutes till the train gets quiet, then I come walking. They may know you got off but they didn't see you.

Robert Lockwood:

Where I grew up, my people was, you could say, middle class livers – everybody had their own farms and stuff, so nobody forced nobody to go to no field. People on both sides of my family had their own little plantations. But I ran into some of that shit in Mississippi, when we got locked up for vagrancy [5].

Mississippi 1973

They would just pick you up — it was a law-breaking thing to not be in the field. They locked us up in Sardis, Mississippi. We did not have to do any work, nothing like that — they really locked us up because in that part of Mississippi they did not have any juke boxes, and they locked us up to hear us play! I understood that after it was all over, they locked us up because they didn't have music and didn't allow juke boxes in Sardis, Como and Batesville. They locked us up because we were sounding very good, and they would take us serenading. They would take us around different places at night, after the people come in from work we would do a lot of serenading, the people would give us money and they would give the money to us. When they turned us out of jail we had over $500 apiece, that was a lot of money at that time. And we were eating in restaurants. It was . . . strange.

Yank Rachell:

You had to know the right people, and deal with the right people. If you had a big man there, nobody would bother his hands. But if you ain't got nobody to fall back on, then, them times they'd do you any kind of way. Unless you fight them or something. And you had to say yessir, nossir. They wanted you to say it to kids who were 15 years old. I was working for a guy, a boss out there on a dairy farm, he had a little old boy name of Pitman. He got to 15 years old and the daddy say, Pitman 15 years old now. I said, yessir. He 15 years old, he want you to call him Mister. I said yessir. I had a brother in law on the farm too, he said I'm gonna call him Pitman, I ain't callin' him no Mister. I said well, time for me to get out. I'm getting out of here. Yeah man, they was a mess down there at that time. That's why so many people left Brownsville, some went to New York and different places. Probably I would have been there now if I hadn't got in a little trouble around there with them.

I left Brownsville because somebody wanted to whup me and I wasn't gonna take no whupping. My momma whupped me enough when I was a baby. It was a guy there, a poor

Talking with the preacher, Bentonia Mississippi 1974

white guy who was a widower. And some girls moved on the farm, they were real nice looking girls, and I was going with one of them. And he was a widower, he wanted to go with one, and wanted me to tell her for him – which I wouldn't tell her nothing for him. So he got mad about that. And he was gonna whup me. And I would drive my car down the highway, and he said, well I'm going on to town and you better not pass me in your car. I was to be playing uptown for a fish fry, and I said well, I'm working up there and playing up there, and I'll have to pass you, if you don't drive but 30 miles an hour – well, you better not pass me.

They had an old gravel road up there, they didn't have no concrete. Well, I had a V8 Ford, and before I got to town he drove side of me and I stopped, 'cause I knowed if I didn't he was gonna try and whup me or something. He said, I told you not to pass me, I said yassuh, he got out, got one of them jacks out of his car, one of them iron jacks, and I got out of my side. But I had a 32 in my dashboard. I just stood there. He said what you gonna do? I said, I'm gonna see what you gonna do, Mr King. He said, I'm gonna whup you. I said, you ain't gonna hit me with that iron. Showed him my gun.

Then he went on to town and told my boss, that nigger of yours, he attempted to shoot me! He said, well, Mr King, he ain't gonna let you whup him with that iron 'cause he work for me, and that car he driving, I bought that for him. That's my hand. So if he scared he('ll) come to my house, and tell me you trying to bother him. That settled that. But I figured I had to leave, so I left Brownsville and went to St Louis.

Chicago street singer Blind Arvella Gray, 1972

Schoolroom, Meridian Mississippi 1974

Lowell Fulson:

I met Texas Alexander in a bar I checked out to hear a little French harp [6]. He asked me to run with him a while, playing guitar. It wasn't even my guitar, it was my ma-in-law's Gibson but she didn't want me to play for the Devil with it! When I got ready to leave town I had to buy my own guitar, went to the pawn shop and got one for three dollars. We struck out and went on.

I liked Tex. We called him Cool Cat. You had to get close to him and say, what you say Tex, to hear him. He talk real slow, real low and deep. He was a good guy. He was a kind of a guy that everything he told you, you believed. What was wrong, what not to do, what to do. He never would look at you, he would look past you – when he looked at you he meant really what he was saying. He was like a big brother or something. Tex liked to keep on moving. He would stay in one place and get restless.

When we got to a new town we would just walk in the place. If a place looked alright to him, he would walk up and start to singing – I haven't picked up the guitar yet – just moaning, groaning, singing. People stop and listening around and what he did, he would take his hat off, and when he'd take his hat off and put his hat down, then I'd pick up my guitar and that was my cue 'cause he was going to work. So we stand around there, and play. They'd be going, Hey Tex, play this. (Mumbles) No. Not enough in the hat to play that. Boy, they'd go to putting nickels, quarters and stuff in there. Mostly Tex sung real old Blues, ones he made up.

Bill Greensmith

Homesick James, Johnny Shines and Howlin' Wolf, 1972

Tex would sing his own songs, then I would come on with a couple. Songs that would, you know, kinda break the nightmare. He liked that. He tried to get me to stay on with him, but I had to go on to Texas.

Johnny Shines:

I went on the road with Robert Johnson after I met him in Hughes, Arkansas, and we took off for the North. Catching rides, hoboing on trains, up through Missouri, St Louis, different places. Get rides with anybody when we were going a short way, hoboing on trains when we were going from city to city. The thing about Robert, any time he was ready to get up and go: didn't have to say but one word and he'd be ready to leave a place. Then we'd get to some place new, check into the town, walk to the black area and start playing on the street, and work out where we would play in the evening – it was never too hard to find out where it was happening. That was how we worked.

Honeyboy Edwards:

Robert used to go with my cousin, but I didn't meet him until about 1937. He was in Greenwood, hustling on the streets and 'fore he left Texas they had released that stuff, and it was selling, like that 'Terraplane Blues' was doing pretty good [7]. He was standing on the corner one Saturday, guitar on his arm, and I come down from the station and by the time I got there some more womens and things got there, and they was drinking, and they didn't know who he was either, they said Mister can you play that guitar, he says I can play a little. She say if you play me 'Terraplane Blues' I give you a dime. He started playing that 'Terraplane Blues' and turning all around and she said, I believe that is that man, that is just like the record. And he said, Miss I told you that was my number. He was pretty famous even before he recorded, but after that he sure enough got out there pretty good. And he always had a woman that had her own house, and cooked – they wasn't making no load of money but they made enough to keep from working, know what I mean? Me and Robert both was like that.

He told me about going to the crossroads. Matter of fact he spoke that he went to the crossroads, and I didn't know exactly at the time what he mean, and what he'd done [8]. But from then on, when I go to the country I went to the crossroads. I come there, sit at the crossroads, get me a bottle of whisky, half a pint, and I sit there play the blues at night, until the sun shine. I went to the crossroads and played and it turned out I got to be a pretty good guitar player. I went through a lot of things to learn some of the things I know. Like when I was young, I'd go to bed at night, and I'd nailed a nail over my bed, and I'd hang my guitar up over my head, and my daddy told me, hang your guitar up there and you won't forget the chords. (Robert) maybe did talk about the crossroads just to frighten people – he said he went down to the crossroads and went down on his knees and met a man, but I never met a man! Robert was a big bullshitter.

Eugene Powell:

One night I was laying down (in) the bed, and that man played the guitar so good. And it wasn't nothing but the Devil, you know. But he was playing that guitar so good, whooeee. Then I woke up. And what I say, I got my guitar that night and played that same piece. I dreamed it. I dreamed one or two pieces. The Devil gave me them.

Guitar Shorty and friend, Elm City North Carolina 1972

Raife Brown, Bentonia Mississippi 1973

Chapter Two - **Notes**

1   Sleepy John Estes. Estes and Rachell worked together from 1919-1927, and recorded together in Memphis in 1929

2   Homesick James recalls working with Fuller frequently throughout the Twenties

3   ie in the Mississippi Delta

4   Mechanical cotton picking machines were perfected around 1945

5   We: Lockwood and Sonny Boy Williamson II (Rice Miller). The two hobo'd together around 1938-40 before establishing the *King Biscuit Time* radio show

6   Texas Alexander, one of the most popular Texas bluesmen of the Thirties, worked with a number of accompanists, including Lonnie Johnson. He and Fulson played together in 1939 and 1940

7   'Terraplane Blues' was recorded in November 1936

8   The crossroads story is a powerful Blues myth: Johnson told Son House that his newly-acquired guitar skills came from a meeting with a 'black man' – the Devil – who tuned his guitar for him. Tommy Johnson was one of several other bluesmen who claimed to have made a similar pact with the Devil

A bar on Chicago's South Side, 1941

BRIGHT LIGHTS, BIG CITY

'Hold on a minute there while I finish my accounts,' says Henry Townsend, flipping through menus on his IBM. He looks younger than his 85 years and, as he saves, hits the print key and quits, I reflect on how the city boy still boasts just a little more sophistication than his country counterpart. A few days before I'd been spending my days on Mississippi porches, chatting and playing for hours with laid back Delta guitarists as the sun went down. It was a different atmosphere here in St Louis, I decided, as Townsend politely told me he could spare exactly one hour, and named a fee for his co-operation. It was a sellers' market, he explained, and write-ups did not pay the bills. Who was I to argue? In his own eyes, Townsend's had more than enough experience of making other people rich, and although he protested frequently that he held no grudges against those folk he believed he'd helped to reach millionaire status, perhaps he protested too frequently. Not to have held a grudge, of course, would have required superhuman detachment.

41

Maxwell Street, Chicago

Relationships between record companies and musicians have generally been fraught. Looking at their history it's not surprising; the first incursions of 'race' record companies into the Blues field were not distinguished with any sensitivity towards artists or audience. Whether urban sophisticates or country farm-boys, the first black recording musicians were consistently portrayed as caricatures dispensing maudlin tales of death or desertion, whilst the first generation of 'race' records recorded in the early Twenties are, by modern standards, insipid affairs. But despite their often heavy handed approach, recording companies such as OKeh, Victor and Paramount went on to document an impressively wide range of music, breaking down regional barriers in the process. Over the same period Blues music moved into larger city venues such as those of the Theatre Owners Booking Agency chain, all of which put on a wide variety of acts including comedians, 'Brownskin models' and dancers as well as Jazz and Blues singers.

The very first Blues recordings were formal affairs, usually performed by female singers from a vaudeville or jazz background, such as Mamie Smith. Generally thought to be the first African-American singer to put the Blues on record, Smith's rendition of Perry Bradford's 'Crazy Blues' was a huge hit for the OKeh label in 1920. Mamie was not a natural Blues singer, but many who followed – notably Bessie Smith – were. From trying to engineer their own Blues hits, many race labels realised that the real thing was preferable, and throughout the Twenties Victor and their like tracked down a wide range of authentic down-home performers, many of them located by talent scouts such as Lester Melrose or HC Speir. As Honeyboy Edwards put it, the scouts 'were riding around the South looking for boys to record. Melrose came from Chicago, and he picked up Tommy McClennan and Robert Petway. He was looking for me but they couldn't find me, I was in Louisiana, so they come on back without me. That's the way I missed that big boom.' Henry Townsend remembers being at the centre of that boom, when cities such as Memphis, St Louis and Chicago were bustling centres for black music, played for both white and black audiences by the likes of Big Bill Broonzy, Bessie Smith, Tampa Red, Ma Rainey and many more. But his recollections of the aftermath lodge even more firmly in his memory, for when the great depression hit in the Thirties, the musicians were among the first to suffer.

Homesick James:

I've worked for gangsters, Mafia, all my damn life. That's why I picked up and learned so fast! I worked with people that, I had to know what time it was. You'd see and you don't see, you'd hear and you don't hear, you know what I'm saying? Talk too much and you know where you'd wind up. I knowed the big guys. I knowed Capone. We worked for him. But those boys wasn't what people say they was – they were much better. One thing, if people can't control you, you ain't no good anyway. If they can control you and put a leash over your neck and lead you around, you's a good boy, but if you tell 'em where you're coming from, that they ain't gonna boss you around, they gonna back off on you. Capone was his own man, and they tried to make him be bad. I think he was alright, he wasn't asking nobody to help him make a living. He did what he felt was right. All good people they gonna say something bad about.

43

I been in Chicago since the Twenties. I never had no problem, when I come in I only had a buffalo nickel and a penny, came in to 12th Street Station, I started playing, somebody came around and said come on with me. I wouldn't know these people, but I wasn't scared of them – I'd turn up and play at any party they asked me. I ain't ever 'feard of nothing – I'm gonna live until it's time for me to go, and that's what time it is. I been places where they been killing people, shooting them down like dogs, but it didn't bother me. Long as they wasn't aiming at me I was cool. I used to play a lot of speakeasies downtown, a hell of a lot. Back in those days I didn't play no black clubs. It was a busy place, boy. Big Bill was one of the first big names, and Lonnie Johnson was there too. But Johnson, he wasn't as big as people say now, that's something they got mixed up. He was a good guitar player but Fuller was rated way over him. Fuller was a monster [1].

I was in Memphis in '38. That's where the people had that place where I recorded, the Peabody, on Union [2]. They had a studio up there, blankets all round to get the sound there, and old wire tape, wire recorders. We had a lot of fun back in them days, me and Buddy Doyle, Walter Horton, we'd get paid for the session and then we thought we were the richest boys in the city! In Memphis there was always something going on, picnics, ball games. And Handy Park was the stomping ground for the Blues. You could find any musician you want there.

I never fancied the women so much. They'd run up at me, but I never fancied them. I'd go out and spend some time with them, but I was too busy gambling and playing the guitar. Womens talk too much for me . . . Yeah, I tell them to their face, too! But that's what it was, a lot of loose women, and they'd gamble too. Bessie Smith, oh now she was a big gambler, I'd gamble with her. Memphis Minnie was a big gambler too. She used to be my girl. We couldn't get along too well. I messed around with her for years. I liked the way she played and sing too, we used to come up with the same ideas at the same time. She was a really good guitar player, and singer too. I just loved . . . but she'd step on you if you let her, she'd rule you and that ain't me – you gotta stop that, now you're barking up the wrong tree, oh no.

One thing about Memphis, there always was a lot of hustlers around. Man, I was good at gambling, that's what I liked. You ask Sunnyland Slim, he was the same. Heck, I was good. I loved to go to parties and things, because always there was a game going on in a room someplace, and when I'd take a break from playing, hell, I'd break everybody out there out of their money, then come back and play a couple of songs and I'd be gone, on to the next place. Cards, crap games, I'd play any kind of cards or any kinds of games there is. They said they couldn't be broke, but I broke 'em. One guy called Blue Thomas, he had a lot of race horses – I won his best horse off him, name of Blue Monday. I gave it to my cousin, said I don't want no damn horse where I'm going, I can't ride him. And he kept the horse till the day it died.

Sunnyland Slim:

Memphis was one of the fastest towns in the world then. Not that it isn't very fast now in a way. Memphis was the fastest thing they had. Now Memphis, I come through there and stayed around 1925, and it was about the biggest town there was for hustling. Gambling, hustling, and all the best-dressed fellas in the world were there.

I know a little bit about the Blues 'cause I run up on a lot of it when I was young, on account of my stepmother. I learned on an organ, the old organ they had back in 1916,

Raeburn Flerlage

Chicago

where you have to pump both feet. I come out of Vance Mississippi, but I never did get to sixth grade. They kept telling me I was gonna kill my stepmother, now I never wanted to kill nobody, but we did never get along. The Blues was really big out there, honky tonk players, and people playing in church – I learned some from Jeff Morris, he was a John Lee Hooker one key man, but I didn't really have no teacher. I was playing for the motion pictures, then me and Little Brother Montgomery had met up in around 1920, and he was some player. It was in Memphis where I started to make a name for myself. Some fellas would be playing in the Park, but not me. I was strictly a club-going guy! They would do all the recording there – they had this white fella come from Chicago to get them on record – Memphis Minnie, Big Joe Williams, fix them up in the hotel and get them to record. That was where I started to make my name, I had this song about the Sunnyland train, they didn't record it but everybody heard it.

You got to hustle. I wasn't the kind of, like the people you have now, who want to kill somebody over a nickel or dime, but I did a lot of different things to make money. On Saturday and Sunday I would play a little piano sometime to make me some money, but there was different things I could do, like making moonshine before I got with Ma Rainey, running joints over in West Memphis, gambling, liquor, cards, craps. And the womens used to follow me wherever I would go. But I don't run around like I used to. I just try to live and be happy. I done did enough running.

Memphis Slim at the 100 Club, London 1960

The Apollo, 125th Street, Harlem, New York City

Jimmie Walker:

I moved to Chicago in 1906, with my mom and dad, and in those years whites lived on the East Side of State Street, blacks lived on the West Side. I went to school at 14th and Wabash – my mother used to walk me over there. There was about six of us going to school there then, but everybody got along alright, we got along fine to my idea. Back then, see, the blacks did not move on the other side of 22nd Street until, oh I guess it must have been just a little before the war – the First World War.

I was about seven years old when I started playing piano. See, a Jewish fella raised me, and I couldn't go in what they called honky tonks, not one of them joints. I had lessons from this boy playing piano, I done forgot what his name was, but I got a hold of him and got him to show me a little on the piano. Well, I was kind of a likeable kid . . . and heck, we went on then, when I heard Bessie Smith and Lonnie Johnson – at that time Lonnie Johnson was playing the violin, a lot of people don't know he played violin with Bessie Smith, when he started playing guitar it must have been around 1914. And I began to pick up a little bit more. I used to play out here when I was still young. I played in Bell House Lounge, I played in the West Side. Homesick and I, we had two jobs at one time. Him and I, we went through a whole lot of crap, man. But I'm still here! Yeah, I'm still here. Another two, three months, if I live to see it, I'll make 90. We always had a good time, no problem. See, I used to run alcohol for Al Capone. I don't even talk about it. You know, I've seen a lot of things, I didn't say nothing, and I made it this far and I don't need to say nothing now. Heck, I could go down this street just like the police, just flying, no stopping at stop lights, no nothing, just keep going and nobody gave me a problem. 'Cause the police knew who I was. And if I was walking, the police would pick me up – pick me up and bring me home! When I got ready to do something, like make a delivery, I'd call the police station, I'd have the stuff sitting right outside and go and load it in the car. I'd have a car full of alcohol, the police are there and people would think they was taking me in. But shoot, I ain't never had no trouble with no police. I was sick one time, and the police was in the house, the lady had let them in, and I thought they said I did something. They come on in and was talking to me, and I said, you just wait a minute, I'll get you out of here. And it turned out they heard I was sick, and had come to take me to the hospital! Shoot, we had some wild times, we'd play for the white folks downtown, but it was really the house rent parties that . . . heck, what they have now is nothing compared with those house rent parties that we had back then . . .

Yank Rachell:

We recorded for RS Peer from New York, a fine looking white fella, in 1929 [3]. What happened was that Lester Melrose and fellas like that would come down every spring and go through the country and find coloured boys, musicians. And they'd get us and set a date for us to come up there and make a record. Like Walter Davis, Sonny Boy Williamson, Roosevelt Sykes, he set a date for us to come, and we'd go up there in Chicago or some part of Illinois and make that record. Or they'd leave Chicago, go through the country and see what they could find, try and catch somebody, ask about who could play music – that's the way they got their money going. In Chicago we made the recordings in a big building, I think about 10 storeys. Then in Memphis they rented a hotel. Not the Peabody, this place was on Exchange and Front Street in Memphis. They didn't have this stuff you have here now where if you make a mistake you can erase it out, and go ahead. If you couldn't have played good you gonna mess that wax up, 'cause they're very expensive.

I only found out later that we didn't get the money we should have, 'cause he give the three of us a thousand dollars. Well I thought the man was crazy giving me that kind of money. I went on Beale Street, some old second-hand store, bought all kind of old suits, wrist watches, then John and I went to Arkansas – the money come easy, we didn't have no sense. We spent it on drinking and having a big time, giving parties, that's all. I'm a young guy from the country, hadn't been nowhere and seen nothing, and when I went to Memphis and made them records that excited me, 'cause I hadn't been used to no money. So I just had a big time – I thought I was having a big time, wasn't doing nothing. If I had got the money I was supposed to get I'd be a millionaire now, but I didn't know how to get it, and didn't have nobody to help me get it. I didn't understand. Since I got older and been around more I learnt that I could have been better off if I'd have knowed how to get it, but I didn't know. When we'd done partying we were broke. It come easy and it went easy. I had to pawn my wristwatch to come back to Brownsville.

Eugene Powell:

Bo Chatmon put me on to the first record I ever made, in 1936. He said I wasn't doing nothing but wasting music, said I'm gonna put you on record. That was Bo Carter, Sam Chatmon's brother [4]. So them were the first ones I ever made in my whole life. Sonny Boy Nelson with Mississippi Matilda and Robert Hill in 1936. It was down in New Orleans. I liked it down there, you know, country boy, had my wife with me, nothing to

49

Roosevelt Sykes at the Chinese Jazz Club, Brighton England 1961

worry about, was giving her a good time, I felt good. I thought I was something, doing something I hadn't never done – I thought I was more than I was! I put out three records for ninety dollars, and that was some money then. And they give me a hundred and something when I was going. With what they give me and all I imagine (I had) around five or six hundred dollars.

We recorded in a hotel. I remember we worked all night. The machine was sitting in the middle of the room, but we was way upstairs in the air, in another part of the house. The place was about seven or eight storeys high, and we was way up there playing music, to be out of the noise and other stuff, cars, or they would get caught on tape – they put those big sheets up over the windows to muffle all that music and stuff. The guys that recorded us, they were nice fellas, they just recorded whatever we wanted to play. They didn't tell us how to do nothing. So we was making some good records.

Henry Townsend:

We were never short of work in St Louis. In terms of how we worked it was similar to what it is now, you had a time to go into your club, you'd be there nine or nine thirty, when people had gathered at the club, and a lot of the time when the musicians get out after leaving the club they'd go out partying for themselves such as a jam. And we'd go out to another place that would stay open 'til the next day and jam and then after that them that wasn't gonna stay there would go home and go to sleep. Then we'd get up early in the evening around five or six o'clock, and start your day off with what was necessary, whatever your tasks was, and then back to the job again.

We had some good musicians in the city – there was the late Leroy Carr and Scrapper Blackwell, Roosevelt Sykes, then you'd get visiting musicians, such as Robert Johnson. I worked with him for a short time – I enjoyed it, wish I'd been with him a little longer. He did have a style that wasn't executed much, though they exaggerated a lot about him, put him up on a pedestal that really he don't belong. It seemed to me that the clubs liked to have a variety. A good musician one night and maybe a less renowned musician the next night because they wouldn't have to pay as much. We'd play clubs and speakeasies. The big clubs were ones like Club Riviera, the Glass Bar and the Cotton Club. Then the other percentage of them were speakeasies. And you would get a lot of whites in some of the clubs in those early days, like the Club Plantation would see-saw between black and white. It always has been here in St Louis, even the dominant black clubs it would be a great percentage of whites coming in – but not the other way around. They treated me, as an entertainer only, like royalty, and out of that I was like any other black male [5].

Things did explode in the music world, everybody was getting money for making records, but I knew it was just a boom, and more or less kept steadfast. Some of the guys that hadn't been around for long blew it, but one thing I would say, those that followed me, or those that were there before me, either way, I just give them credit for being there, because there is so many of us that has made so many millionaires and we are not, and that's pathetic. The record companies made a fortune, namely that guy Melrose who mainly dealt with the blacks, he made him a fortune, and on and on – Columbia made a fortune, RCA made a fortune [6]. And the people actually responsible for this coming to be didn't get nothing. That's the part that kinda hits your mind and hurts you a little. I kinda held on and accepted a lot of things – there's absolutely nothing that I could do about it, so why not accept it? Make it comfortable for yourself. That's the way I see it.

Guitarist 'Satan' with 'Professor Six Million' on bathtub bass,
125th Street, Harlem, NYC 1982

Chapter 3 - **Notes**

1   Fuller: Blind Boy Fuller. Homesick's assertion is debatable – Lonnie Johnson was more successful as a recording artist than Fuller

2   According to Homesick James, he recorded for the Victor and Vocalion labels in 1937 and 1939

3   Rachell recorded several songs with Sleepy John Estes for RCA Victor in 1929, including 'Diving Duck Blues' and 'The Girl I Love'

4   Bo Carter, aka Armenter [Bo] Chatmon, was one of the many musically-talented sons of violinist Henderson Chatmon. Brothers Sam and Lonnie later played together in the Mississippi Sheiks, with whom Bo occasionally guested: the Sheiks' 'Sitting On Top Of The World' would become an early Delta classic

5   ie whites

6   Lester Melrose became a talent scout after helping sign Tampa Red to Paramount; he later went on to work for RCA and Columbia

KING BISCUIT TIME

Delta Broadcasting Inc / KFFA

Sonny Payne gathers up his cartridges and locks up his records as he concludes one more *King Biscuit Time* show. It's over 50 years since the one-time Western Swing bass player started working for KFFA, but as we walk out together into the Helena sunshine, chatting about Decca valve microphones and horizontal polarisation, it's obvious that radio will always remain an obsession for him: 'Can't get it out of my blood. Wouldn't want to.'

Guitarist and harmonica-playing barber Wade Walton in his shop, Clarksdale Mississippi 1988

Delta Broadcasting Inc / KFFA

Joe Willie Wilkens | Joe "Pine Top" Perkins | Sonny Boy Williamson | Mr. Hugh Smith Announcer | James "Peck" Curtis | Houston Stackhouse

King Biscuit Time

Radio wasn't a new invention when Sonny Payne first started broadcasting. But black radio was. Before *King Biscuit Time* the new forms of Hillbilly music that were epitomised by the Carter family had been popularised by the radio – in comparison, black music was overlooked. KFFA, launched just a few months before, was typical of a local station, playing a mixture of Benny Goodman and Harry James, along with a smattering of Gospel, when Rice Miller approached the station's Sam Anderson with the idea of his own show. Miller needed a sponsor, who materialised in the shape of Max Moore from the Interstate Grocery, and *King Biscuit Time* was born. The show would make the small town of Helena, already a popular location for Blues musicians, the focus of a whole musical community, anticipating what would happen in Chicago at the end of the decade.

The centre of this community, Rice Miller, remains a mystery to many people. Miller had hobo'd around the country with Robert Lockwood throughout the Thirties, and took to using the name Sonny Boy Williamson around the time he started performing on the radio, apparently to cash in on the reputation of John Lee 'Sonny Boy' Williamson, the nation's best-known harp player. The two had already met when Miller started using Williamson's name, but apparently Williamson, an easy-going character who collected comic books as a hobby, regarded the imitation as flattery. According to Billy Boy Arnold, who knew Williamson in the Forties, 'when Miller was broadcasting on the King Biscuit show the announcer would say

"OK now, go out and get some Sonny Boy flour and go out to the record shop and get a bunch of Sonny Boy's records", but Rice Miller didn't make any records until 1951. So whose records did they get? Sonny Boy didn't suffer. He just thought, "Let him go ahead, if it makes him a dollar, let him make it" – he didn't have any hard feelings against Rice Miller.'

Miller himself was a hard-bitten professional who'd been with Robert Johnson on the night the latter died. A keen gambler, Miller cultivated a rough exterior, but most of his colleagues had the greatest of respect for his abilities as an entertainer. According to Payne 'if the guy had a fault it was that he'd look after other people before he looked after himself. He was charming to work with. Sometimes on the show, of course, you'd announce a song and he would go on to play a different one, but that was just his way.' Placed by virtue of his show at the centre of the Delta's musical scene, Miller gave many local players their first break – and inspired many more. Just as significantly, Miller's great collaborator, Robert Lockwood Jr, was the first Delta player to explore the possibilities of the electric guitar. Although electric Blues will always be associated with the bustling streets of South and West Side Chicago, the seeds were sown in the rather more small-town surroundings of KFFA's studio above the Floyd Truck Lines building, overlooking the Mississippi.

Sonny Payne:

Helena always was a wide open gambling town. I was born and raised here, and we had slot machines on every corner, in every business and every cafe. Even though it was still illegal they did this in order to build a hospital, which we desperately needed. At the time Helena would be the first stop for the steamboats going down the river from Memphis to New Orleans, so this was quite a large river town – wild and wide open.

King Biscuit flour came on the market in 1931, but it didn't really take off until Sonny Boy Williamson and Robert Lockwood came to Sam Anderson. They'd heard the Delta Rhythm Boys on the radio and wanted to do their own show. Max Moore came up with the idea of calling it the *King Biscuit Time* show, and that's what it's been ever since. It began in 1941, and just took off like nothing else ever took, for the simple reason that some people heard music that they had never heard before – yet on the other hand some people who lived in the country, on farms and plantations, they had heard it and knew what it was and what it meant. Because we didn't have too much interference we could go anywhere from 75 to 100 miles in four directions – which you can't do today – so the show would reach a huge audience. Radio was still in its infancy back in those days, even though it went on the air in the Twenties and Thirties, but the reaction was fabulous. The show went out live. We had one microphone, hanging from a boom, for the two of them, and Sonny Boy would play his harp, and Robert Junior would play guitar. Back in those days they knew how to make microphones, the sound was so powerful. He played his gig and enjoyed it very much. I think that show really opened up the area. It was really the start of everybody appreciating Afro-American culture.

Robert Lockwood:

Rice Miller was about the first guy I'd go off playing with, we'd go off all over Mississippi, all over Arkansas, down to Gulfport Mississippi, back up all over Arkansas and a whole lot of Tennessee – up to Brownsville and several other cities I done forgot the name of.

We'd be two or three months away from home. And I'd come home with all my money – I wasn't no hell of a gambler, not like Rice Miller. It was after I went up to St Louis and Chicago, did some recording, when I got back to Helena, that was when the King Biscuit thing started. It was the old man who came up with the idea of the radio show, he dragged me along with him, so we went to Anderson, and he told us to fix up a sponsor, and we came up with King Biscuit flour too. Started off with the two of us, then after a while I hired Peck Curtis, and bought him some drums, and we'd get out and play on the road as well. We got to be pretty popular, and it kept us pretty busy, but then the money kept coming up wrong and all that shit, and I quit, started working for Mothers Best flour and put together my first band [1]. After I left, that's when they started getting a whole load of different people on the King Biscuit show.

James Cotton:

Meeting Sonny Boy was the best thing that ever happened to me. I picked his thing up from the radio, and I met him when I was about nine or ten, and started playing with him. He was about the biggest thing in that area at the time. I liked being around him – I picked up on everything he did. He was a very moody person, but if you knowed him, you got on good – I respected him, he taught me everything I know. It was Sonny Boy brought me to West Memphis, and we used to do *King Biscuit Time* together in the Forties – that was really what started me off. Then Sonny Boy went to Wisconsin and gave me the band, but we didn't stay together, 'cause I was too young. They had people like Joe Willie Wilkins, Willie Love, Willie Nix was the drummer and all these people was trying to be band leaders, and I was just a crazy kid. Couldn't keep them together.

Little Milton:

The first time I remember hearing Blues on the radio it was Sonny Boy's radio show. Whenever the batteries weren't down I'd listen to *King Biscuit Time*, out of Helena Arkansas. Then it wound up that Rice Miller was one of the guys that really taught me the business. Playing with him – I never recorded on a record – he taught me self-esteem, he taught me respect, taught me how to not only respect yourself but to respect the audience – 'cause without the audience you were nothing. And Rice Miller was a hell of a musician as far as the harmonica was concerned. He's the first guy I ever saw who could blow the harmonica through the nose, through the corner of his mouth, he had all sorts of gimmicks he could do! He was a very kind-hearted gentlemen, he talked loud, and he had a big bluff going and if you didn't get to know him you would think, whoa, this guy's mean, he's vulgar . . . but deep down he was really a gentle soul. But he knew what he wanted – he was in charge and he would tell you what to play and how to play it, and if you didn't he'd be on your butt. He would stop in the middle of a tune and tell you to get it right. He was just that way.

It was a few years later I got to be on the radio too. Some kind of way we had started doing broadcasting, and I think it was one of the owners of the stations, WGVM in Greenville, had noticed that I read pretty well, and that my diction was pretty good. So they called me in the office one day and asked, would I be interested in doing a radio show as a jock? And they could get me a sponsor. 'Cause what I was doing was paying for my own time, they let my band play 15 or 20 minutes on the air, then I would announce where I was gonna be.

Michael Ochs / London Features International

Little Milton

CeDell Davis:

This area has always been strong for the Blues. Nobody here knew of any other music but the Blues. The reason is the living conditions, you know how things were back then, or you may have read about it. They would write songs about women, dogs, chickens, cows, trains, cars, airplanes, buses – anything you could lay into a Blues singer they would write a song about it. Living conditions and everything. Blues tells a story. Rock music don't do that. When I was growing up, everybody who was a musician wanted to get on that show. I played on there in 1951 or '52 with Houston Stackhouse, James Curtis, all of them. I wasn't on the payroll, but you can guess what the payroll was. I was working with Robert, so I didn't get paid for doing the show, but I'd make my money when we went out and played [2].

BB King:

I got one of my first breaks through Sonny Boy Williamson's radio show. I was staying with Bukka White, and I happened to turn on the radio one day and heard Sonny Boy's show in West Memphis, right by where I was [3]. I had never met the man, but I went over there and asked him if I could do a tune, and it turned out pretty well, believe it or not. Then it turned out that Sonny Boy had a regular night at this place, the 16th Street Grill, but he'd lined himself up a night at another place that was paying more money. So Sonny Boy called the lady that owned it and she let me play one night in his place. Then when I played there she told me if I could get a show on the radio like Sonny Boy she would let me play every week, for 12 dollars a week – and I'd never earned that kind of money before! That was how I came to work for WDIA. I had my own show for about three and a half years, sponsored by Peptikon. Sonny Boy used to advertise a tonic called Hadacol, and Peptikon was a kind of rival to his product. It was supposed to cure just about everything . . . I think they had quite a lot of alcohol in there . . . So I started off with about 10 minutes a day, and ended up with two 55-minute shows, plus a live 15 minute programme, where I would play with my band. And of course we got to advertise where we were playing. That's how a lot of people got to hear about me.

Robert Lockwood:

I was one of the first guitar players to have a pickup in the South. I got my first one, a De Armond, around 1939, from the Montgomery Ward catalogue [4]. Me and Charlie (Christian) was riding along close together – Charlie started putting his stuff on records about 1939 or 1940. I would have loved to meet him, he was so young, I think even younger then me – the guitar wasn't even in the race at all until Charlie Christian. Shortly after that they started making the guitar with the pickup in them, and I started buying them. I had a guitar with a pickup as long as I was on *King Biscuit Time*, then I started to work for Mothers Best, and I went to Memphis and joined the union, and I think my first electric guitar I got from a pawn shop there, I think it was a Gretsch. When I went back to Chicago again everybody was pretty excited by the idea of the electric guitar. I was fortunate enough, I invented a lot of the things, a lot of the new styles, like playing with harmonica players and stuff like that.

Jimmy Rogers:

When I was growing up I heard Lonnie Johnson, Memphis Minnie, Tampa Red, Big Maceo, people like that, on records – my uncle would get the records, he had one of those wind up Victrolas, so it was in my mind I would like to do some of the things those guys are doing. Then later I met guys like Walter Davis, St Louis Jimmy, and Joe Willie Wilkin from the King Biscuit things not too far from Memphis, and that's when I finally got the chance to see those guys in person – like Sonny Boy, Rice Miller. He was the biggest singer in the area – a fine gentleman, only thing was that Joe Willie and Robert Jr would complain to me that he loved to gamble, and if he blew his money at the crap table sometimes they don't get paid. Robert Jr Lockwood was one guitar player I really admired, then Joe Willie Wilkin from Memphis was a guitar player I'd really taken to because he was more in my age bracket – he was more my equal than Robert, and when I met him he was using a De Armond pickup on his guitar in Memphis. That was the first electric guitar I remember seeing. That was what gave me the idea for putting a pickup on my guitar.

Sonny Boy Williamson II (Rice Miller), Fairfield Hall, Croydon England 1963

Bill Greensmith

60

Robert Jr Lockwood 1972

Sunday night, Bentonia Mississippi 1973

Sunday night, Bentonia Mississippi 1973

Chapter 4 - **Notes**

1   Robert Lockwood Jr led his own show, the *Mothers Best Flour Hour*, on KFFA from 1943

2   Robert: Robert Nighthawk. Houston Stackhouse – Rice Miller's guitarist after Lockwood's departure – and Nighthawk played for several KFFA shows including *King Biscuit Time* and *Mother's Best Flour Hour*

3   BB is referring to Rice Miller's radio show for KWEM in West Memphis, sponsored by Hadacol tonic

4   The electric guitar was invented around 1932 but did not become readily available until around 1936. The first electric players simply added a pickup, such as a De Armond, to their regular guitar. Charlie Christian, an inspired Jazz player, popularized the electric via his work with Benny Goodman and early Bop sessions at Minton's in New York

HOW BLUE CAN YOU GET?

Sitting back in an over-padded leather recliner, Lowell Fulson takes a sip of coffee and lights up one of his cheroots. He's what you'd call a cool cat. It's not the two chunky gold rings on each hand, the air-brushed nude on the wall, or the Italian suit; It's the fact that Fulson is as mellow as a vintage malt. The king-size TV in his room is relaying the worst Democrat returns to Congress in decades, but despite the playful efforts of Tina Mayfield, with whom he stays, to needle the 73-year old guitarist about his party's downfall, there are no cracks in his laid-back demeanour. As Fulson relates stories of confrontations with racist cops, how he gave away the publishing to 'Three O'Clock Blues', or how he sold a priceless Gibson L-5 guitar for just a couple of hundred bucks, the closest he gets to anger is a kind of urbane puzzlement. Equally, when I tell him that Eric Clapton has just recorded Fulson's 'Reconsider Baby' on an album that will inevitably be a huge hit, Lowell only utters the slightest of murmurs at the thought of the thousands of dollars headed for his bank account before asking: 'What kind of cat is that guy? Can he sing the Blues?'

63

Margie Evans and Lowell Fulson, Los Angeles 1976

Fulson and many of his contemporaries weren't the impoverished sharecroppers of popular legend. They were entertainers. The twin mentors of Fulson and BB King were essentially T-Bone Walker and Louis Jordan, for Walker was the first to show the musical possibilities offered by an electric guitar and a small horn section, while Jordan's version of 'Jump Blues' brought a new sophistication and humour to Blues writing. Although Fulson and King both started out playing the traditional Blues of Bukka White or Texas Alexander, T-Bone Walker inspired them to explore the tonal palette offered by combining the electric guitar with a horn section. Along the way they created a form of music that was distinct from either Delta or Chicago Blues, and which would have its own distinct influence on the Rock 'n' Roll, R&B and Soul music that followed. Fulson, King, Little Milton, Bobby Bland, Ray Charles, and other performers who followed them profited from a new eclecticism, partly fostered by the recording boom led by newly-established independent record companies. Although many of their tricks were learned first-hand in church, or in the musical hot houses of Memphis or Helena, they also absorbed influences from the likes of Charlie Christian, Django Reinhardt or Bob Wills and his Texas Playboys, directly from the vinyl. As a result they wrote intelligent, slick pop songs, which bear little relation to many of the tired and predictable retreads that pass for Blues, forty years later.

The slick suits, too, don't match the preconceptions, as I find when I'm ushered into a dressing room at London's Albert Hall for an interview – an audience – with BB King. Time constraints and the ministerings of BB's camp followers force me to conduct the interview jointly with the editor of a rival magazine. Contemplating the difficulty of establishing a rapport in a three-way chat, I shudder as my colleague opens his questioning in a puzzled manner, looking around at the plush carpets, the Louis Quatorze chair, the gold plated Lucille and, yes, the suit. For God's sake, at least Eric Clapton and Jeff Beck have the decency to wear jeans in such a situation. 'All of this,' he enquires, 'can you really play the Blues with all of this around you?'

BB's smile is benevolent, and there's no clue as to what thoughts of 40 years of grinding touring, totalled buses and restaurant service via the back door pass through his mind. Then the smile turns into a laugh, a big boisterous laugh, and he contents himself with a one word reply.

'Yes. Next question.'

Little Milton:

Every guitar player has tried at one time or another to sound like T-Bone Walker, and that bars none – BB King, yours truly, you name 'em. To me he set a style and example that there's no way you could play the so-called progressive Blues without touching, somewhere in there, T-Bone Walker. I just don't think it can be done. It's like a trumpet player trying to play a trumpet and trying not to play a note of Louis Armstrong or WC Handy. It's literally impossible. He was the first guy to play single note solos, he used those Jazz chords, and his guitar accompanied his voice. He literally made the guitar sing to me, and talk to me. And most of the guitar players of that era were just chording, playing back-beat bass and stuff like that. I don't mean that they weren't that great, but his stuff spoke to me in a more sophisticated way. I been classified as a blues guitarist, blues singer, which is fine with me, 'cause the music I've done, I've loved it and I still do.

T-Bone Walker at 'Jazz Expo 1968', the Gaumont Theatre, Hammersmith, London

S.P. Leary playing with the Muddy Waters band at the 'Jazz Expo 1968'

And they can call me anything they want as long as they don't call me late for dinner. But I've always had a thing about standing on a stage doing a full night of doing nothing but 12-bar blues – that would bore me. And T-Bone's style, or people like Percy Mayfield that did different things, that meant I could let myself out into different pastures.

When I finally got a chance to play with T-Bone I was thrilled to death. And I tell you, the day I was scheduled to meet him, I got there real early to make sure I'd see him. There was him and his chauffeur in this big Cadillac and man, you would have thought I was a woman waiting for a man that she admired to show up, I was just so excited! We had big laughs about different things, we set in the dressing room and got the guitars, and he showed me several things, and we really got to know each other. A few years later we got to be very decent friends. And he was a very intelligent guy. Some people, they think that all blues entertainers has got to be . . . non-educated, semi-educated, filthy, raggety, evil, broken-hearted, living in poverty, that they live the life they sing about. This is not true. This is definitely not true, this is a wrong concept.

SP Leary:

Bone was my main man. He taught me the way to go, he was my instruction, he was my everything, 'cause I couldn't even go to any place unless he come to my home and pick me up – I was too young. When I was playing with Bone I was about 14 – I couldn't go too far, but wherever he took me I'd go. Furthest was Oklahoma City and back to Dallas. That was about 1944, 45.

He was already playing electric guitar when I met him. That's all I know. I never known him to perform with an acoustic guitar. But he was the man with the guitar far as I'm concerned. Just ask anybody that ever worked him. He could do everything, he was a showman – he had a show along with his beautiful guitar playing, and never missed a stroke. Played it behind his legs, between his legs, used to hold his guitar flat across his chest, man, and pick it, behind his head and everything. T-Bone used to dance too. He was a dresser, everybody knew that. And he knew how to keep a big band together. As far as the music, he knew exactly what he wanted. He knew exactly what you could do, how far you could go, that's why he hired you. And the songs he wrote, they would mean something – they have a meaning, a story behind it. His songs may just seem simple to some people, but they don't stop and listen to what he's saying. If you listen – the man is telling you something, he been through this. He's trying to pass on to you what not to do, or what to do.

Lowell Fulson:

I got discharged from the navy on 7th December 1945, and in April '46, right after my birthday, I came back out to Oakland. I was down on West 8th Street when I heard music going. So I went on over there, followed where the music was. There was a little old record pressing machine, and there was this guy Bob Geddins pressing his records. I said, hey, how are you doing? He looks over, how you doing, alright, sit over there – I got to get these records out here. He had one of them one horse machines, as we called 'em – couldn't press but one record at a time.

They had an old guitar sitting there, beat up, and I picked it up and went to playing and singing. The press stopped. Ain't you that singer that was here eight months ago? I said yeah, I was here. He said, you remember talking to a man said he was gonna record you? I said, don't know what I'm gonna do, I just got in town. Did you ever cut a record? I said no. Do you want to make a record? – I'll give you a hundred dollars. I said, yeah. He said wait a minute, see if I can get someone to run this press – can you cut now? I said, right now. So I went and cut, and that was when I cut 'Miss Katie Lee' and 'Black Widow Spider Blues'. I didn't cut but two. 'Black Widow Spider' like to have made a hit – if he had had international advertising, it would have been everywhere. He would take the records and put them in the trunk, it would be full in the back seat and on the floor on up, he would be gone in the morning, half a day and he would have sold every one of them records. Just pressing them up and selling them himself, one man operation. But I wasn't getting nowhere, so I quit fooling with him. But that's how I got to be known in the recording business, is from Bob Geddins. He was the man [1].

Johnny Vincent:

I was running a little record distributing company when I ran into Art Rupe and Specialty Records. I'd sell to all the juke box operators, and I got to know all the hits because all the jukebox operators would come back and tell me what record was playing on their jukebox. I'd cut several artists and they were local hits, and Art Rupe wanted me to find guys to record, promised me a deal where I'd get one cent a record for each guy I cut. Rupe was a very sophisticated guy – he never did want to get down and get with the working class. He wouldn't go in the rough joints, so he put me to doing it. He was high class, a writer, wrote for Jack Benny or somebody, and went into the record business 'cause he had all this money saved up.

It wasn't no disadvantage being with a small label. It was an advantage, because we were eating good with our record company. We didn't have the money Columbia had, because those guys had a catalogue of Dick Haymes, Guy Lombardo, Johnny Mathis or whoever it was. They didn't want to fool with black music 'cause it didn't do the volume enough to be profitable. So that's why you had the companies like Chess, Vee Jay, Trumpet, you had a lot of little companies started out. You had the Bihari Brothers, who had the back end of their car with the tape recorder and they would go into the Delta to record, and then they latched on to BB King, and I think BB just liked them and stayed with them. Then Chess were out of Chicago and they were hungry and they would do basically the same thing – Leonard would get in his car and put 2000 records in the trunk and he'd come down and sell them to little shops like me for cash, he'd cut that stuff for $50 and press them up and put a thousand or two in his car, sell them in Memphis, Jackson and then he'd go maybe to Detroit and do the same there, five or six hundred. We knew what records would sell, knew what would sell 40 or 50,000. In fact we knew better what would sell in those days then we do now, 'cause you didn't have the different facets of music to worry about. Sure it was good fun. If it wasn't good fun we'd have got out of it.

BB King:

There were a lot of good guitar players to listen to when I was growing up! It was Lonnie Johnson that I hear some of my lines from, and then there was T-Bone, who started off the whole single note thing, put Jazz chords into the Blues. I once tried playing bottleneck guitar, but I've always been something of a thickhead, and it took me enough time learning the guitar without learning the different tunings! But I loved the sound of the vibrato Bukka White would get, and I guess I was trying to get a sound like that, but with just a normal guitar.

I never did seem to have too much luck with record companies when I started out. Seemed like I was putting them all out of business – I did four sides for Bullet, out of Nashville Tennessee, then they went out of business. I thought my records must have been so bad that it was me put them out of business! After that I went with the Bihari Brothers, Modern Records, on their subsidiary label, RPM. Then when they decided to put albums out, my first one was on Crown, another subsidiary of theirs, then they changed me from Crown to Kent. Crown was a kind of cheap grade where you could buy a record for 98 cents, then Kent was a little better, and would have a bit of a better way into the market. Modern were OK people, with the Biharis it was like a family thing, you could always call up and talk to them. But the albums made by the major companies were graded higher – it wasn't just the price, it was the quality of the record, and where

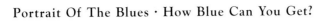

Jukebox, Bentonia Mississippi 1973

B.B. King on the road in Connecticut 1975

you could buy it. On the smaller labels, even if you had a big record it wasn't graded to where it could get in the Top Ten. That used to bother me. Then after the first few years, about the time the Rock 'n' Roll thing became big, it became very difficult – hard to get records on the radio. The only way to get the people to hear your records was to go out and play. Get your own bus and get out on the road. So that was when I bought my first bus and started out, and you could say I've been on the road ever since.

There were hard times, but I can't remember any time when I thought I couldn't go on. To me, I had it easy compared with working on a plantation. Of course I'd get tired. I remember once when I lost a guitar 'cause of it. I've lost lots of guitars, but this time was definitely the worst. I'd been playing a club and I was so tired when I was driving home that I would pull up outside my apartment, shut my engine off and go to sleep in my car, 'cause I'm too tired to go up to my room. So one night I'm asleep in the front seat, and I don't know it but the car door is open in the back and all of a sudden I hear (brushes his guitar string). I wake up and there's a guy taking the guitar out! The guy out-run me, I was running like a guy running for his life, I threw a brick at him and hit him, he did a flip but kept on running. I couldn't catch him. That had to be the worst way I ever lost a guitar! The way it woke me up, I guess Lucille was saying, he's taking me!

The B.B. King band on the road, Connecticut 1975

71

Lowell Fulson:

With 'Reconsider Baby' they wanted me to cut it up in Chicago, and I had to tell him that I wanted to do it with my own band and record it ourselves, 'cause they could really understand what I was trying to do. We had a big band, seven pieces, one of the best bands that was touring in the country. At least until Ray Charles took them off me [2]. They was so tight.

When we went through the South we had to be careful – most of the boys hadn't been South, so I lectured to them. Told them how to go about ordering food, where to go in the restaurant, where it says Coloured. Didn't have no trouble but once. That time they wanted to beat that trumpet player to death because he wouldn't say yessuh, nossuh.

What happened was, my bus and this passenger car was meeting each other on a bridge – it was wide enough but if you were not an experienced driver it guess it would look pretty small and this other car ended up half on the bridge, half off it. Then suddenly here come these sheriffs, four sheriffs. They got there so quickly it looked like they was already there. But what really frightened me was them guys coming out of the woods. I call them kind of diehard guys. I said, don't nobody get off the bus, just sit here till the sheriff come. Sheriff walks up. Who did this, where is the bus driver? I said, don't nobody move. He

Pianists Cousin Joe Pleasant and Otis Spann, London 1964

72

went round taking names – who saw what, where was you sitting? So he's talking to Flemmy Nesque. Now Flemmy is a Carolina man, from the South, but he won't say yessuh nossuh. We're trying to tell him, we're looking at him, trying to get him to say it, but he won't say yessuh, nossuh. So the police guy snatched him off the bus and shouted, do you know how much it costs me to kill you? A nickel. That's what the shell costs – a nickel. I was lucky, calmed him down by telling the sheriff, sorry sir, he is a little retarded, he is a good musician, but he just doesn't know. He said, just get back on the bus. Wham, turned us loose, and we're out of there.

Tommy Ridgley:

One time with Buddy in Shreveport, we played the Country Club. At the front you had steps like you were going upstairs [3]. Buddy was in his car and he got there ahead of me and the policeman tells him to go to the back door. And Buddy gets mad, he won't go in no back door, so I came up there. I knew something was wrong. I go to Buddy, what is the matter, he's saying, he telling me to go to the back blah blah blah. And I'm looking over there, the policeman had his hand on his gun, but he just didn't say anything. So I

Brownie McGee (left), bassist Ransom Knowling (hat and shades), and Muddy Waters at the rear with hat on, London 1964

went over there and asked what happened. He said, nothing, all I did was tell him to go round the back, 'cause there's a ramp that goes straight to the bandstand. That way you don't have to carry all the equipment up the stairs...

Chapter 5 – Notes

1   Bob Geddins was one of the first African Americans to run an independent record company. Jimmy McCracklin was one of his other major discoveries.

2   Several of Fulson's key sidemen went on to play with Ray Charles, notably saxophone player David 'Fathead' Newman.

3   Buddy: Buddy Williams

SWEET HOME CHICAGO

'I wouldn't say everybody in Chicago was crooked. But there were a lot of people on the take. You could walk round all night, have a drink in every club and you wouldn't have covered the lot of them by the morning. And there were a lot of palms greased to keep them open that long. As for the record companies, well there weren't many of them who cared that much about their musicians once they walked out of the studio. None of them, Leonard Chess or anybody else, thought that later on there'd be people who thought that period would be part of history, or that there'd be English kids studying every note of that music. In fact I'm sure they didn't.'
Bassist and songwriter Willie Dixon chuckles for a moment.

'And I have to admit, I didn't either.'

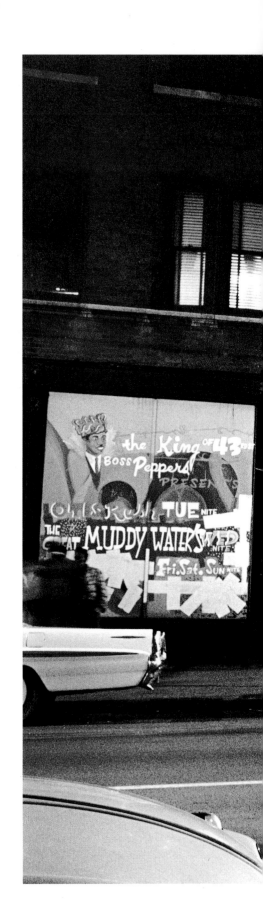

Outside Peppers Lounge, 43rd Street, Chicago

The explosion of talented Blues musicians in the Chicago of the Fifties seems incredible in retrospect, a product of the movement of huge numbers of migrants from the southern states, and the presence of more than a few inspired individuals. Chicago wasn't alone in being the destination of black farmers from the south – huge numbers of migrants from Mississippi, Alabama and Tennessee were moving to industrial cities such as Detroit, Pittsburgh and Chicago from the end of the first world war. But Chicago was unique in its vibrant and occasionally violent nightlife, which was largely the legacy of William 'Big Bill' Hale, Chicago's Republican Mayor. Bill Hale was, ironically, voted in on a reform platform, but the Chicago gangs prospered under his regime, and a network of speakeasies, brothels and night clubs soon extended throughout the South Side of Chicago. Work in the stockyards and steelmills was plentiful, thanks to the halting of immigration in the First World War, and as Dixon put it, 'they worked hard, and they played hard too. Everybody was busier than hell. It was all happening round the clock, parties, shift work, men and women hustling... it was just the greatest town for musicians!' Chicago's clubs teemed with jazz and blues, and the demand for musicians was unrelenting, drawing in the likes of Lonnie Johnson, Memphis Minnie and Big Bill Broonzy in the inter-war period. Together with John Lee Williamson, who effectively established the Blues harmonica as a viable instrument with hits such as 1937's 'Good Morning Little Schoolgirl', these acoustic players ruled Chicago. But with the end of the Second World War, a new electric order was set to conquer the city.

Willie Dixon was one of the few established players to prosper in this new era. As I listen to stories, narrated in the warm croaky voice familiar from his records, it becomes obvious why. Even now, constructing grandiose schemes, analysing record production, or telling how he got one over on a rival, his grandchildren's rap records blasting out in the background, Dixon is the definitive operator. The man's skills as a prototype A&R man and producer are undeniable, but it is probably his knack for talent for wheeling and dealing that sets him apart. For the architect of some of the greatest moments in popular music, spine-tingling songs performed by Otis Rush, Muddy Waters or Howlin' Wolf, there was more to Chicago than just music: 'I'd be lying if I said we didn't have to put up with lots of bullshit, just trying to get hold of the money we earned. And there was the bullshit that came from the rivalries you had between different musicians. But we knew how to have fun. To really have fun. It was like having a party for ten years of your life.'

Buddy Guy:

When I was a kid I would listen to the music on the radio station, Rambling Records, out of Memphis Tennessee, and they'd be playing John Lee Hooker, Muddy Waters and early Howlin' Wolf – and it seemed like all of that stuff was coming out of Chicago. It seemed like there was nowhere else you could go if you wanted to play music.

I was a sharecropper's son in Louisiana, and those were bad days. We couldn't afford any air conditioning or anything like that, but my mother had a screen on one door to keep the insects out, and that's what I made my guitar strings out of. I'd take a kerosene can, nail a stick in and stretch the wires across there. You couldn't finger it, but I'd just bang away on it. Now my daddy and his friends would see me play this thing and they'd say to themselves, well, if that boy had a guitar, I'm sure he would learn to play. Then when I was

Muddy Waters performing at Peppers Lounge, Chicago, with Jimmy Cotton

about 16 my daddy saw a relative who sold him a guitar that only had two strings on it, for around a couple of dollars.

It seems like my life has always been built around surprises, 'cause when I left home I went to high school and was living with my sister for a year, and I used to sit out on her porch playing this beat-up guitar. Now one Friday afternoon this stranger passed and said, son, I've seen you sit there a couple of days with this guitar. Now you don't know me, but I've seen you need strings and everything, and I bet if you had a new guitar you would play it, too. And I said, I don't know what I would do, but I'd sleep with it and never let it out of my hands. So the guy said, you be sitting here tomorrow evening, and we'll go and get you a new guitar. Sure enough, I was sitting there the next day, this guy comes up, says, let's go, and I followed him downtown and he bought me a brand new guitar, brought me back and sat me on the porch. My sister came in, we all started drinking and getting high, and my sister said, let's have some fun – we got a country boy, a guitar and a car – let's go out into the country. So we stayed up and had fun all weekend. But from that day I never saw that guy again, and I wish I could find him, 'cause that guitar cost 52 dollars, which was a lot of money in those days.

After that I would play with a lot of guys who would come to Louisiana, Lazy Lester, Slim Harpo and some more, but I knew I had to do something better. So I explained to my mom and dad, I'm gonna take off and go to Chicago. Seems to me it's better there.

So I took off on the train, and when I got off the train I just had my guitar and two suits of clothes. I didn't know anybody there. So I would walk around, didn't have nothing to eat, and stayed hungry into my third day, so hungry I was about to cry, when this other surprise happened. This stranger came up to me and said, you got a guitar there – can you play that thing? I said yeah, and he said, well if you play me a song we'll get some drinking done. I said, if you buy me a hamburger or something to eat I'll play all night for you. And he said, I don't buy no food man – I don't know where you from but we're just gonna drink now!

So I tote my bag and I'm trying not to cry, and I knew my mother was going to worry if she knew what shape I was in. But I'd seen those old Western movies and thought, well, if I take this drink of whisky at least I'll have some strength, something to keep me going for another day. So I took the first drink of whisky I ever had, and man, my eyes flipped around four or five times, and every song I ever knew, and some I didn't, I could play.
So we're at this man's house, and we's just jammin', and this guy says, Jesus Christ man, we got to go where someone can hear us. So we walked to this club about four or five blocks away. This particular night was Otis Rush night, and evidently this guy knew Otis. Now the guy who owned the club was in to pick up the take, and on his way out I played him 'The Things I Used To Do' by Guitar Slim, and this guy turned around and said to the manager, whoever that guy is, hire him. So the manager says, you can come in Tuesday, Wednesday and Thursday – have you got a band? I said, sure, I was that desperate to play. I had to go back the next night and say to the manager, look, I'm just new from Louisiana, and I ain't got a band. He told me, we'll get a band, you just be here, and he came over with Fred Below, a drummer. I didn't have a bass player or nothing.

Then the second night I was playing there I looks out in the audience, and there is Muddy Waters, and Little Walter, and I thought , Oh Jesus, what am I going to do now? But I knew I had to do something good, 'cause now that I'd seen these guys, I was never going to go back to Louisiana [1].

Buddy Guy on 'Ready Steady Go!' TV programme, London 1965

Billy Boy Arnold:

Everybody came from Arkansas, Mississippi, and Georgia to Chicago to get the jobs. The Blues came from all of these places, so that's why the clubs in Chicago survived, because there was the audience for it. They worked at the factories, the steel mills, the laundries or as chauffeurs, whatever menial jobs they had. When they got through on the weekend it was worth working all week for the little money they made because they knew, man I'm gonna hear Big Bill tonight, Sonny Boy is playing down there tonight. You know you'd go and hear Sonny Boy, and you were free from the pressures of the South. You were in a black environment, hearing your type of music. So that the cities were always stronger for Blues, because you had a collective of people there, whereas when you went down South there was a lot of people in the country who liked Blues, but the younger people, they often wanted to hear something a little more up beat.

Jr Wells:

My father didn't have an education. All he knew about was sharecropping. He was in a plantation called Jimmy Kerr's, down in . . . I can't recall the name, and I don't never want to recall it no more anyway. He worked all the year plying mules, the man give him land for him to build his own crop on, and at the end of the year he' supposed to have done made about five hundred dollars for that year, which he spent at the boss man's grocery store, on lard, molasses, cornmeal, flour, things like this. But he was happy. Onliest time he learned how to write his name is when I showed it to him. But he did me a favour because one day Mr Jimmy Kerr told him, that boy you got there got big enough to do a thing now – we don't want him laying around, I want to see him in the field tomorrow. My daddy said, you got to talk to Emma, this is his great grandmother. So he went and told my great grandmother, I want to see that boy in the field tomorrow. She said no, our little boy won't be there, he said, I'm not disputing your word but I want to see him in the field tomorrow.

They took a wagon, Jimmy Kerr's was about 12 miles back in the woods off of 51 Highway, they took me on a wagon out there and got me on a Tri State bus. To Chicago, to my mama's.

Raeburn Flerlage

Junior Wells at Theresa's, Chicago

Harmonica player Big John Wrencher and band, Maxwell Street market, Chicago 1972

Jimmy Rogers:

My grandmother reared me, and where she'd go I would go. She had two brothers, one lived in Detroit and one was in Chicago, and she could get tickets to travel by train – anything like that they'd send her tickets. Chicago was where I started meeting guys I liked and was really interested in. She had me in St Louis for a while, and I met Walter Davis down there and St Louis Jimmy. Then I'd met guys like Joe Willie Wilkin from the King Biscuit things not too far from Memphis, and that's why I got the chance to see those guys in person. Sonny Boy, Rice Miller – I had already met John Lee. Then I met Little Walter and we was playing around together in Memphis and Helena.

I came on a bus. Chicago to me was just another big city. I'd been around Memphis and places, and I knew you had to stay on your toes and watch the people you associate with. I had uncles and cousins in Chicago, so I felt pretty safe there. It was a big raggety city to me, big tall buildings, cars blowing their horns, buses running and people making a lot of noise. But I wanted to meet these guys: Tampa Red Big Bill, Memphis Slim, Memphis Minnie, Doctor Clayton and people like that, 'cause they were based around there.

Me and Blue Smitty, Lee Brown, Baby Face Leroy, we got a little band together. It wasn't too hot but we played little local gigs – they call em chitlin' gigs, but we was out there havin' fun, workin a day job. On Saturdays we'd play out on the street. They done tore that all up now, you go down there and all the hot dog stands is gone, the clothing stores, and all that is gone – Jewtown's not Jewtown any more [2]. So that's where we started

Big John Wrencher and band, Maxwell Steet market, Chicago 1972

up, playing in the street to make a little money. That was real fun, they'd throw money in the kitty, and really on weekends, Saturdays and Sundays, from maybe around 11 o'clock to about five in the evening, you could make more money like that with three or four guys just playing and collecting money, for those couple of days, than you could make in a club in the whole week!

Joe Willie Wilkin had the first electric guitar I'd actually seen, in Memphis. So when I got to Chicago I got a guitar with a De Armond pickup, and put it on there so we had an electric sound. We had just small amplifiers, I had a small Gibson with a 12 inch speaker, but you could get a good sound. That was before Muddy came. So it wasn't hard to get him hooked in to wantin' to hear that sound when he got to Chicago, to get him a rig. We'd get the power from a man that was in the block, he would drop an extension cord down from his front window down to the street, and we'd jack in there and get the juice. Right there would just be our group, then down the street there'd be someone else doing the same thing.

Now those other guys would be playing acoustic, but the sound of the amplifiers was drawing most of the people away, so we would make good money – that's why we did that. Man, there's be hundreds of people around, some give you a quarter, 15 cents here and there, whatever, as they pass the kitty, and we'd make in a day, split it up, and you'd make 60, 70 dollars each or maybe a little more sometimes. And in a club you'd only get four or five bucks a night.

Raeburn Flerlage

Clubland audience, Chicago

Muddy Waters came to Chicago in 1945. His cousin Jessie Jones was always round where we'd play. Muddy was down at Clarksdale, and Jessie said I have a cousin that's coming to Chicago, that was around March or April, so when he did get there I met him, and we talked. And Muddy was a kind of a shy guy of big cities – and he wouldn't get around too much. He'd talk to people if they talked to him, go to work, come home, and that was it. But Blue Smitty and I talked to him and he decided he'd come and play with us, so he got interested in this deal. When Muddy came in, he had a hollow f-curve guitar like Gene Autry's, I think a Gretsch, and there was a place in Chicago where I knew we could get a pickup which would fit that type of guitar, so we took him to 18th and Halsted and got him a De Armond pickup put on his guitar, and a little amplifier, and then it sound loud.

We'd play around different places in Chicago, house parties and little small clubs, maybe Friday Saturday and Sunday once in a while. Then Sunnyland Slim would come around, and Sunnyland was a old hustler back at that time, into a lot of stuff, shoot pool, dice, cards and he was a piano player. Then he brought Little Walter to Chicago from St Louis, and I introduced Walter to Muddy as a harmonica player, 'cause I was playing harmonica and guitar as well. So we got together, rehearsing, playing little house parties, stuff like that, people liked it, then Jessie Jones got us a little night-club deal, tavern I would say, not too far from where he lived, on Roosevelt Road. People come in, liked what we were doing and it went from there, started building up, got bigger and we got something going. That's how the band got started.

Sunnyland Slim:

The old Sonny Boy, that's little Sonny Boy, I got on with him and Big Bill Broonzy pretty well when I came to Chicago. They wanted me to stay here, but I had a house in Carruthersville, one out in the country and one in town. That's where Little Walter used to hang out. In fact I had been to Chicago a whole lot of times, I played with Memphis Slim, that had to be in the early Thirties. I had been playing up in Wisconsin somewhere, I was playing up there but I wasn't getting no big money. So I came back here, and was playing with Tampa Red, Big Bill, Lonnie Johnson used to help me a little bit.

Chess had been worrying me about doing some recording for some time. I had been playing with Lonnie Johnson, but he was in prison. And Johnny Shines was out of town. It was my wife had the idea of using Muddy on guitar.

Me and my cousin went up to his house — we took the street car and walked all the way

Sunnyland Slim   Johnny Embry (guitar), Maxwell Street, Chicago 1972

from 18th St to Canal, and we had to wait on him to get off. He was driving a pick up truck, and told his boss he had to go to a funeral. I helped a lot of people start out – I'm thankful I was able to do it. [3]

Billy Boy Arnold:

In 1948 the major artists on the scene and in the record shops were Big Bill Broonzy, John Lee Williamson, Memphis Minnie, Louis Jordan, Charles Brown, Arthur Crudup, T-Bone Walker, Brownie and Sonny, Walter Davis, Memphis Slim, Willie Dixon and the Big Three Trio. Those were the guys that were on the scene, and just about that time Muddy Waters and Lightning Hopkins, made their first records, and over the next few years, by around 1950, there was a total change in the scene – a total change. The electric sound had taken over. I remember seeing Memphis Minnie around Chicago in 1953. She was still playing in clubs but she didn't have the popularity, because Muddy Waters had taken over, Elmore James had come on the scene with 'Dust My Broom', Little Walter was on the scene, Jimmy Rogers had a few pretty good hits, Howlin' Wolf had made a major impact, Guitar Slim was coming in there, BB King had made his big thing around '50 or some time like that, so it was new names – and Big Bill Broonzy and those guys who had been on the scene for 30 years were fading out.

Bruce Iglauer:

In terms of blues there's a specific traditional reason why independent record companies were at the heart of the music. Before World War II there weren't very many record companies; a lot of them failed during the depression, and the distribution of records was very limited – it was owned by Columbia and Decca or RCA. Another thing about the

Giving thanks where due – BB King, Connecticut 1975   Willie Dixon, Fairfield Hall, Croydon England 1963

record business then that was interesting, was it was a record business in which there were no Jews – it was very restricted. The recording of blues after World War II began very much on a street level, people like Bernie Abrams, who ran Ora Nelle Records down on Maxwell Street, who listened to bands playing outside his store and thought, if someone wants to listen to this stuff on the street they might want to take it home. Because of the control of real estate interests, especially in Chicago, the Jews were at the bottom of the white people barrel. Apartments were very restricted, and what happened is, first you had the white Anglo-Saxon Protestants then the next step down were the Bohemians, then the Irish, then the Poles …I don't know the exact order – it's the order of immigration, the longer you've been here, the more legitimate you are. The Jewish neighbourhoods later became black neighbourhoods, because after they let the evil Jews in they could allow the really evil blacks in. Because the Jewish neighbourhoods and black

85

Under the 'El', 63rd Street, Chicago

Under the 'El', 63rd Street, Chicago

neighbourhoods grew up side by side there was a lot of interaction there. That's why a lot of the early post-war independent record people were Jewish entrepreneurs often who were in other businesses, like the Chesses, who were in the night-club business within the black community.

Jimmy Rogers:

Muddy started out recording with Sunnyland and Big Crawford on bass. The reason Leonard wanted it that way; Lightnin' Hopkins he was playing by himself, John Lee Hooker was in Detroit playing by himself – he wanted small music with an outstanding sound. Now Muddy didn't like to play by himself like that, he thought that there was something missing and he couldn't get the sound he wanted. To me it sounded OK. They were one of the first records with electric guitar on, in Chicago.

More and more people was comin' into the clubs, and we started getting pubs taverns that would take maybe 75 people full capacity, then they started moving things around and got more space, then they started putting a charge on the door, you'd pay a dollar at the door and get one beer, then they put a straight dollar charge on, then we started moving to bigger clubs and it went from there on up. The thing turned out to be real big. Then we started recording together, Muddy refused to do records without us. At that

63rd Street, Chicago 1972

time we didn't have a bass player, and we used Big Crawford a while, he wasn't with the unit but he'd come into the studio and bump upright bass on some of the stuff, then Willie Dixon got in with Chess.

That was when we were really experimenting live, if a guy came in and we thought he was pretty good we'd let him sit in. And he'd sit in and play, then when we'd get ready to record if one of those guys had something to offer we'd use him and he'd love to play, wasn't any money but he'd just play.

Buddy Guy:

The clubs then, you had a shift of people who would get off at 11 o'clock at night, and the average club here didn't close until four in the morning. You could go Monday, Tuesday and Wednesday night, and 3.30 in the morning your place was packed. Then they closed at four, then you had another shift of people got off at 7 o'clock in the morning. We used to have what you call a Blue Monday jam, when we would start playing at 7 o'clock in the morning and you could not get in no club we played in. You wouldn't believe it. It was a round the clock thing, the city buses was running all night and people could ride the public transportation all night.

63rd Street, Chicago 1972

You had Theresa's, you had Pepper's Lounge, you had Smitty's and that was just a few of them – there was a thousand night clubs here, some of them didn't hold but 40 people, but that's just how many people would be in there when you got in. A lot of people was working then, we had the stockyard here going 24 hours a day, the steel mill was running 24 hours a day, and I actually lived in Chicago for about five years and lost track of which was the weekend. I had to ask somebody which was Saturday, which was Sunday, 'cause every night the clubs was all full, every night Buddy Guy was walking down the street trying to find someone I could learn from. They had the late Earl Hooker, LC McKinley, Freddy King, Magic Sam, I could name so many guitar players, horn players, harmonica players. I'd go looking for them and you'd pass this little joint next door with no name, and you walk in there and go, wow, who is this? And they was playing as well as the guy you were gonna see.

Eddie Burns:

I was based in Detroit when I played with John Lee Hooker. He was about the Blues-est thing in the city. We used to come over and play in Chicago a lot. The two places were completely different. Detroit never was 100 per cent blues – maybe Chicago wasn't either – but Chicago is more like Mississippi than Detroit is. Detroit, you always did have

Under the 'El' 63rd Street, Chicago

Theresa's, Chicago South Side 1971

other kinds of music here other than Blues – you'd hear bebop, swing, standards like Duke Ellington. In Detroit the musicians didn't all like playing Blues. But in Chicago they really liked that Mississippi thing.

Hubert Sumlin:

Put it like this, the atmosphere in Memphis was kind of like that in Arkansas, Louisiana, Texas everywhere – they were bluesy people. They had Arkansas blues – but they was playing the same thing that people did in Louisiana. This is where all the stuff began. I believe it just migrated to Chicago from these different places. I know I did, I was born in Mississippi, raised in Arkansas. I think Mississippi had some of the best Blues musicians you could get, Louisiana, Mississippi, Arkansas, Tennessee – Chicago just got into the thing when everybody started leaving and migrating and coming to Chicago. I don't know too many people, too many musicians that was born in Chicago.

In Memphis, you had one street, the main street, this is where the music was at, but in Chicago you had the South Side, North Side, East Side, West Side – when I got to Chicago you could go out of one tenement so fast and get to another band, it wouldn't take you two minutes out the door into another door. When all the musicians came from the South, we made Chicago. We made it 'cause we had more music than anybody. But it was

Hubert Sumlin, Fairfield Hall, Croydon England 1964

just a big old city, man, people played everywhere. Big lights, big city, like Jimmy Reed said. I heard so much about Chicago before I even got there, you know how it is, people who had been up there come back and say, hey man, it is too bad up there, people shooting one another, they doing this, doing that – watch yourself. I said, well, I am going anyway. So hey, I got to Chicago – and they learnt me fast. My first pay cheque, the first week that I worked there, I got stuck up.

Somebody, when I first got to Chicago, said, hey you gonna have to have a gun. I said, oh no man, I don't need a gun. Oh yes, I bet you, everybody got a gun. I said all right, so he sold me this 38, automatic I believe – yeah, it was an automatic, man, heh heh heh, a great big old long black automatic. Shoot nine times, had a clip, nine times, and he said, I am going to show you how it works, so we went out in the country, me and this guy did, he just shot this old shack, tore this shack all down and I said, yeah man, I'll take it.

It was on 47th street there in Chicago. We played the 708 Club, we got the end of the week coming, and they all knows I done got paid 'cause they comes to see me. It was three guys, three youngsters – but they was as big as me. I had a pocket-full of money, my whole week's salary, one got on this side of the street, one got in the middle of the street, one got on the other side of the street. I got out of 708 Club with my stuff, I had my guitar in this hand, I didn't have my amp because I got to walk home. Man, that was the longest walk. Them guys didn't close to me until I got ready to make the bend, 'till I got ready to go Chess's building, so then they all come across me, gonna block me off. I said, hey guys, I don't know what you all looking for this morning man, I said, but you guys gonna get hurt. One pulled out a long knife, I don't know how long, but that knife looked to me like it was as long as I was tall. I just pulled out my gun, man. Pow, pow pow! The gun scared me, man, but it scared them more – these guys tickled me, one went that way, one went that way, one went that way. I laughed all the way home, with my guitar and gun all the way into the building. When I got inside, I thought, what am I going with a gun out in Chicago, and put it back in my pocket. I got up there, Wolf done gone to bed, but I couldn't wait to tell him, I woke him up. I told him that these guys tried to stick me up a while ago . . . I scared them though. He said, maybe you won't be bothered with them no more. I said I hope not. It tickled me so bad, I went to sleep laughing, thinking about these guys, how they run.

I figured that was it. I figured I had done conquered Chicago. But I didn't. The next time they got me, man, I went to get off the bus, and there were five little kids, one ranging from six or seven years old, and the oldest one was about 13. And the littlest one had the shotgun, sawn off shotgun, big as he was, and he just unzipped it some kind of way and come out with the shotgun, put it on me, and I had just got off the bus.

Mister, we know who you is, all we want is your money. Get out your shoes, then you pull off your pants and then everything else you got on. I mean quick. This is the little old boy with a shotgun. The others just standing there, yeah, do like he say. I did. I did it, man. Folks were coming by, walking by me, then when they saw me naked, everybody went to go the other way, thataway! I didn't have but 14 cents, 14 cents, and they said, this is all you got? I said, that's all, y'all, I said, now go ahead on and kill me. That's all I got. I was so scared . . . then I heard somebody, a voice, saying what are you all doing? I said, I hope he doesn't scare them and make these dudes kill me. It was the little old kids' man. Here come their daddy, boy he take the shotgun from the little one, line them up man, line them up, beside the wall. He said Mister Sumlin, I am sorry about this, very sorry about this. I said you ain't as sorry as I am. I was putting on my clothes, getting them clothes on, 'cause all the folks was watching, it was a big old scene, and he said, what they do? I said they taken 14 cents, that is all I had. He gave me 14 cents. He give me my 14 cents back, and he said to the kids, you look at him good, he live two blocks from you, he said, and if I ever hear tell you put a hand on him or do anything about him but help him get home, I am going to kill all you. Yes sir, yes sir. I had no more trouble. When I left from that place, that was the quietest place in all of Chicago.

Chapter 6 – Notes

1:   Guy has compacted events which took place over several weeks to several days in this recollection

2:   Jewtown: Maxwell Street, the celebrated street market which was the city's most popular venue for buskers.

3:   Sunnyland is referring here to bringing Waters along to a recording session for Chess in 1947. Leonard Chess decided to record Waters as the front-man for two songs, including 'Little Anna Mae'. Waters' next excursion into the studio in April 1948 would produce what is generally cited as the first electric Chicago Blues record, 'I Can't Be Satisfied'.

CHESS MASTERS

'This is it, my den, man,' says Hubert Sumlin as he ushers me into the basement. It's Hubert's music room, a treasure trove of memorabilia – hundreds of photos line the walls, wooden shelves are packed with CDs and tapes, and a fluffy black and white cat sprawls across one of three squashy sofas. 'His name's Lucky – he loves musicians,' says Hubert, shifting him to an adjacent cushion as he settles down and sifts through his CD collection. 'Can you believe that they brought all this stuff out again, man? Somebody did some good research here.' Charley Patton or Robert Johnson records that he bought on shellac 78s in the Forties are present here as lavish box sets; his own career is similarly documented via Chess collections of Howlin' Wolf, Muddy Waters, or Chuck Berry CDs. This afternoon, he's scheduled to attend a ceremony celebrating a set of postage stamps commemorating Wolf and Muddy. 'I never would have thought it would have happened, not in a million years, but, hey, I am glad it did. Not only Wolf, but Muddy and everybody else, they paid their dues and this is something that really is going to help the youth. To help the young generation to think, people you never thought would have made it, they made it, and they taught you things.'

Albert King, Hammersmith Gaumont, London 1969

The gulf which Howlin Wolf and Sumlin crossed was in some respects a relatively short one – a musical and geographical jump from Mississippi to Chicago. But although both Wolf, Muddy Waters and others had grown up on the music of Charley Patton, the music they produced was far more than simply an electrified version of Delta Blues, and would effectively become a prototype for the Rock music of the Sixties. Fifteen years before Eric Clapton discovered the potential of distorting his guitar sound to give more harmonics and sustain, Little Walter was obtaining the same results with a small Silvertone amplifier.

Many of the musical advances in Chicago were technologically driven, as musicians unleashed the potential of new electric instruments and amplification. Rather than being the instinctive musicians of popular legend, performers such as Sumlin, Freddy King or Little Walter worked industriously at learning new techniques or sounds, and demonstrated that an all-electric band could be more effective, more musically mobile than its big band competition. Their musical discoveries would be carefully studied by British musicians of the next decade. It's no coincidence that the sound of the ultimate late Fifties blues band, fronted by Howlin' Wolf, based around distinctive rhythms and catchy over-amplified guitar riffs, would effectively constitute a primer for the ultimate late Sixties rock band – Led Zeppelin.

Sitting with Hubert in his basement, it's hard to imagine him in the cut-throat musical arena of Fifties Chicago, where it wasn't unusual to arrive at a session and find your employers trying out another guitarist to see if he could out-do you. For this is a man who delights in self-mocking stories, such as how he was sacked by Wolf because he couldn't learn the riff for 'Smokestack Lightning'. Then you realise that Sumlin's secret lies in realising that it isn't always easy making great records. Sometimes it's plain hard.

'You can get one song, a hundred different ways, man, before you find what the song is all about - is somebody is telling a story, who did this, did somebody kill somebody, why they do that? You gotta think about what you're saying, and it better fit. And you got to have your instrument together and your voice together, and it's gotta be where somebody feel it, where there is going to be some soul there. This is what it is all about. If you can get that together in two hours, one hour, you're alright... you's a genius, I think!'

Jimmy Rogers:

When Muddy put his electric on it was a bigger sound, stronger, people could hear it was different, and they went for it. Muddy was nine years older than I, and he was trying to do Robert Johnson's sound with the steel on his hand, the slide, and I understood what he was trying to do and I could support him on that level. So after I got in there with him, me and Baby Face Leroy was playing the heavy stuff and he could just run like he wanted with his slide. And we had this thing, I don't care how far you range in the room, just meet me in the corner! That's how we got it together. Blue Smitty, he was a pretty nice guitar player, but he was mostly hung up on his job, so he dropped out and Muddy and I, we just kept on doing it. It was Little Walter, Muddy and myself, then we got Elgin Evans and Baby Face Leroy, so we kept on – that was my shot, that's all I wanted to do.

When we were recording for Chess, Leonard was the boss. With Sonny Boy, Muddy, me, Wolf, he would be trying like he was producing. I guess he was trying to get the best out

Howlin' Wolf, Fairfield Hall, Croydon England 1964

of it in his own mind, regardless if he was interfering or mixing up our ideas. We were out there in the public, playing for them, and what we would hear and put together we'd take to the studio, and he would want to change it. Sometimes he'd come up with a good number that way, sometimes he'd blow it – it was a very complicated situation. The first one we recorded, we had to get in the union, and it was 41 dollars in the quarter. There were four sides to make one session – we got the 41 dollars for the quarter out of the session, and so we didn't get no money. He put the record out and you'd hear it, and I'd paid my dues and got my union card and that was it. He didn't have no mercy on you out of the record sales.

We'd do a session and I would say we generally have the studio for three hours. Leonard would pay 75 dollars an hour for rent of the studio, he had his own engineer, Stu Black, and we'd go in for three hours and do as much as he could squeeze in, one record after another, trying to pile in all he could. You didn't even have time to concentrate. Sometimes we'd throw something together and let it pass – to his opinion it was OK, but to ours it wasn't, but we let it pass. Then he'd put it on the shelf, take one recording out of the four and releases it.

Howlin' Wolf and Muddy Waters didn't see eye to eye too well, 'cause there's a jealousy situation. Muddy wanted to be the big bear, Wolf wanted to be big – nobody was getting too close to Chess but they was thinking one would outdo the other one. Chess would get Muddy cars every two years, and take it off his royalties. Wolf would get his own car, wouldn't let Chess buy one for him. Wolf was in the Pontiac situation, Muddy would deal with Chevys – it was about who was biggest, who was the big dog. Guys making all this money – it was childish stuff they be doing. Really Wolf was better managing a bunch of people than Muddy was – Muddy would go along with the company, Wolf would speak up for himself. And when you speak up for himself, you automatically gonna speak up for the band, because if you don't agree to record, there's no recording. It was more of a business thing with Wolf.

Black Wall of Pride, Atlanta Georgia

Otis Spann and an Irish fan, Fairfield Hall, Croydon England 1964

Robert Lockwood Jr:

Chess got involved with me because I was a very valuable source – everyone wanted me to play on their records, and it just happened like that. I was with Chess for 11 or 12 years. But the reason why they didn't record me under my own name was that I knew too much. You see I would listen to what Chess did with other people's records, they paid a man to stop playing them and all that shit, or else some guys who recorded for Chess, he wouldn't release it, just leave it on the shelf and let the guy suffer. I told him a couple of times, if you do me like that, I will blow your motherfucking head off! He knew I was very serious. That's why he never would record me.

Hubert Sumlin:

Wolf sent out to me from Arkansas. I was staying with James Cotton, at this old hotel in West Memphis. He said, Hubert, I'm putting this band down and I'm going to Chicago and form me a new group, 'cause these guys, they think they're too good. I said okay. Like that. I didn't believe him. I really didn't believe him. And so Cotton said, hey man, when he said he was gonna take you to Chicago, do you know he meant what he said? I said, I hope he do – I would like to play with the guy. Sure enough, two weeks later, he calls up the hotel, the train leaves at so and so time and you are going to be met by Otis Spann, Muddy Waters' piano player. I said thank you. Sure enough, that's what happened. I packed my little suitcase, got to 12th Station, Otis Spann met me, and took me on back to my apartment. We stayed in Chess's daddy's apartment building. Wolf had an apartment there, he got me an apartment and had done got my union card and everything. He already did all of this for me when I got there. That second day, me and Wolf we had done had lunch and everything, sitting down, and he was beginning to tell me what he was doing, how this worked, when he started playing, and what and what, then we start to sitting around, me and him playing on guitar, going over the numbers. And I got to like that old man. I was kind of scared of him at first, he was go big and huge, but hey, that didn't last long. He was just like a little baby if anybody knowed him.

Willie Dixon:

The Chess brothers always told me they were gonna start a company and when they did they wanted me to play with them. I thought they was just kidding, but sure enough they called me up. The first thing I did for Chess was playing string bass on a Robert Nighthawk song – 'Sweet Black Angel'. After that I ended up on a whole lot of sessions – Muddy, Little Walter, Wolf, Eddie Boyd, Chuck Berry... really, I was playing bass on most of those records until they came up with the electric bass.

Leonard Chess called himself the producer but he didn't really know what was going on. He never knew nothing about no music – if you made a record he could tap his foot to, he'd think that was a good record. A lot of times he'd just antagonise people in the studio, swearing at them 'cause he thought that would make them play better. We'd waste a lot of time that way. He was smart latching onto Blues because it made him money, but he never had much of a feel for the music itself – and if he had ideas he didn't know how to explain them. But after a while he started to listen to me because I'd tell him when I thought a song wasn't going to sell. After one or two of my things went over OK, he began to have confidence in me. He was smart enough to surround himself with guys who knew what they was doing.

A lot of people think the Blues is just 12 bars – but it don't have to be 12 bars. Some musicians don't understand that either, they wanted to do the same songs all the time, but you have to explain that, if you're doing something different, the songs are gonna stick in the audience's mind. You need to make a different kind of sound for it to go over, with a different introduction, a different rhythm, a different way of expressing it. And you got to have a theme to your record. 'Hoochie Coochie Man', that's from the old idea of the seventh son of a seventh son, how he has special powers. Or some lines people can remember, like 'you can't judge a book by looking at its cover'.

I had to get involved in the recording, to get the right tone, otherwise it wouldn't come out the way I wanted. Getting the sound was sometimes hard. There was this rivalry between Wolf and Muddy, and each of them thought the other was getting the best songs. A lot of times Wolf wouldn't like a song unless I told him I'd written it for Muddy. Little Walter didn't want to do 'My Babe' – I knew it was right for him, but it took me two years to get him to record it, and it turned out to be his biggest hit. It was sometimes difficult, but I'd go backwards, forwards, any way I could to get them over. In the studio, it was a question of blending the sound. You got each of the guys only thinking about what they are playing, but you got to be thinking about how all comes together, and how it will come out on record. There was no headphones, maybe only one or two microphones, you'd have to do all the harmonising and blending with your ears, go into the room and listen, and work out how to blend the sound properly.

Willie Dixon, Fairfield Hall, Croydon England 1963

Little Walter, London 1964

I wouldn't say that Chess appreciated what I was doing. I got fed up with money coming out wrong, that's why I started working for Eli [1]. I'd brought Otis Rush to Leonard – Leonard told me he didn't need another Muddy Waters. Muddy Waters, Otis Rush, he couldn't tell the difference. Then Eli gambled away all the money he was making, and I had to go back to Chess. At that time I didn't know enough about copyrights – you might get one check from Leonard when he felt like it, then you never knew when the next one was coming. One time Willie Mabon thought he had a big cheque coming from Leonard after he had a hit with 'I Don't Know', then when the money arrived it came up short. He went into the Chess building with a gun and Leonard had to lock himself in his room. Chuck Berry might have had enough clout to go after Leonard with a gun, but not Willie Mabon. He ended up getting tied up in knots with the lawyers.

SP Leary:

I worked with, recorded with, quite a few different artists, Elmore James, Homesick James, Snooky Pryor as well as Muddy and Wolf. That's where I got my style from, 'cause each one of these guys, they wanted a different stroke, a different beat. Muddy had the contract with Chess. They contact Muddy, and Muddy gets the boys together – doesn't matter what time it was, we'd go. It wasn't a hassle. If Muddy had an idea he wanted to get it together then, before it get off his mind, or whatever. Willie Dixon was involved, very much so, he was a hell of a guy and a composer. He'd explain what to do, correct it right away, tell you this is how it's supposed to go. You know he wrote for just about everybody else, especially in the Blues field.

The side man like myself, naturally you want to be pleased with your performance, but you got to have it like the top three want it – Muddy Waters, Chess, Willie Dixon or whoever else was in charge of the session. You a sideman, man, you doing the job. Play that music the way they want it played.

Keep doing it 'till they get it right like they want. Then you got to satisfy Chess, if they ain't satisfied then it ain't going nowhere, and then Willie Dixon, then the artist . . . all three of them got to be pleased.

Koko Taylor:

Me and my husband, Pops Taylor, we got a Greyhound bus, didn't have but 35 cents between the two of us, and came to Chicago. I got a job working for rich white people, cleaning their house, taking care of their kids, washing and ironing their clothes, and scrubbing floors on my knees. That's how I made a living. It was hard work, but it made a tough, honest woman out of me. My husband and I start visiting a local club and we finds all of these people working here and working there, Muddy Waters and all of them, and my husband told everybody, he let them know, my wife loves to sing, and so the guys start calling me up to jam with them. Now this was for no money or nothing, this was for my own pleasure, my own enjoyment. Sitting in with different bands and all of this, Willie Dixon happened to be in the audience one of the times and he came over to me and said, my God, I never heard a woman sing the blues like you sing the blues, he said, this is what the world need today – more women. He said, we got plenty of men but no womens and he wanted to know if I was recording for anybody and I said no, so it was Willie Dixon that took me down to Chess records. That's where I did my very first recording, under the jurisdiction of Willie Dixon. It's a man's world and it's not that easy getting into it, but he wrote my first song and got me recorded, he wrote for me 'Wang Dang Doodle', and that was my biggest break. He was very specific, very direct and very outgoing, outspoken, he was a man he knew what he wanted – he demanded that, no more and no less – this is how I want you to do it, I know you can do it, so open your mouth, close your eyes and get with it.

James Cotton:

Once I started recording with Muddy, we lived in Muddy's building in Chicago, one of the rooms was on the first floor, I lived on the second floor, and Otis Spann, he lived in the basement. Otis had two rooms, bathroom, kitchen and bedroom and the piano out in the hall. And that's where Dixon used to come over and bring the words to what he wrote. Otis would sing them and play the piano. And Muddy, who was up the stairs over us, would be in the bed listening. And that was how Muddy actually learned the songs. Everyday we'd see one another. But we had complications. For the longest time Muddy had this little room in the house with a half bed, that's where he slept at in the daytime, then him and his wife slept out in the back at night. Now I used to play little solos, and he'd get mad with me, say, that's the wrongest shit I ever heard in my life. Then I'd bring the record and put it on and it was exactly the same!

Koko Taylor at the 'Jazz Expo', Hammersmith Gaumont, London 1967

Jimmy Rogers:

Muddy said I think we should try to make this thing an all star unit, so next time we go in the studio we gonna demand that Walter play on a number and put his name on a record. So next time we went in that's what we did. We had maybe 15 minutes after we did my session, and we said we wanted to hear this number that in later years was called 'Juke'. At the time we called it 'The Jam', we'd do it coming on stage and also during the intermission, we'd do a couple of verses of this number and take a break. So people'd know when we're opening up and when we stopped – it was our theme song. So we thought we'd try what it sounded like. So in this 15 minutes we got Stu Black to let us put it on tape. Leonard was clearing up and getting his paperwork together and it caught his ear, so he gets on the speaker and says what is that? So we get it on tape and then we all got real excited.

Otis Spann

Jimmy Cotton

Then we left, we went to Shreveport Louisiana, we had a tour with John Lee Hooker, and Walter came with us. The first week we're down there that's the first damn record we heard on the jukebox across the street from where we're staying. They had a speaker on the outside of the door, so when you play a record in jukeboxes you can hear it out in the yard. We heard this thing, I say that sounds like us, man – can't be, must be some Louisiana guy. We went over there, walked in, and went to check the jukebox to see what the hell's going on. We looked and looked, then finally somebody punched it, the number was on there, we went down and looked for that number on the list, and it was Little Walter and the Four Jukes. And we said Four Jukes, who's that? But it sounded good. Then Walter got ideas. Walter played with us about three more days, and he called Chicago and talked to his old lady, Al Benson was the DJ in Chicago and he's pumping it.

Then Walter left us in Shreveport, then went and picked up Dave and Louis Myers and Fred Below, that's the Jukes, and left Junior in the street!

Dave Myers:

People think me and my brother Louis were cotton field Blues players. But we shook up the city, boy. When we started out here in the Forties, all the music in the city was big band, swing music. We used to hang around with this swing player, Lee Cooper – he got us enthused, and told us to get into the music, to learn it, and sent us down to this big store, Lyon and Healy, where they had a lot of good teachers [2]. And that's where we started out, learned our scales, learned to play bit by bit. When the Aces got going, no one in Chicago could touch us, man. We were some of the first guys in the city to use pick ups on our guitars, in 1945. And we were about the first guys in the city to use Gibson guitars – I was using this old L-5 until a fat lady sat on it. And I was the first guy in the city to play an electric bass. When they brought the first one in the city, to 18th and Halsted, they gave me the first Fender Precision bass – said, we know you got a feel for this, take it and see what you can do with it [3]. Then the Fender guys came down with the first piggy back amp they had in the city. When I took that, that blew out just everybody. I hooked that son of a gun up, we hit the road, and everywhere we went I destroyed them upright bass players. We be playing up against big old swing bands with horn players, and we just had our guitars and the harp. We destroyed them. The guys was so amazed. It was a thing, man. Everybody in the city – they was terrified of us, man.

Hubert Sumlin:

I left Wolf and went with Muddy for one reason – Muddy gave me triple the money Wolf was paying. You know how it is when you young, you see the money and that's all! He sent his chauffeur over in his Cadillac and the chauffeur had on diamonds and everything and I am looking at this big roll of money – I ain't saw so much money in all my days. Muddy done sent him over to bribe me, man. We was at the Zanzibar, on intermission, he say Muddy sent me over to tell you, he triple the money that Wolf paying you – what do you want to do? He ain't talked to Wolf or nothing. I told him, yeah man, alright I'll do it, so I go and now I'm gonna have to tell Wolf I'm gonna go with Muddy. So I goes in the bathroom, guy done gone back to Sylvio's, but I still got his money – oh man, I had about 400 and something dollars. I had more money than I ever seen in my life. So I got this money and it is 10 minutes before we get ready to go back to the bandstand. Now this place is full of folk, jammed, and this bathroom didn't hold but two, the man's bathroom. So I got in that bathroom to count my money and to think about what I am going to tell him. Shoot man, Wolf come in there, he done change colours – he got blacker! This guy got a ton of colour I ain't never seen a man turn. I say, oh shit, how can I tell this guy, man. But I didn't have to tell him, he said, look, I heard that you wanna go to Muddy. I ain't gonna hold you down, I'm gonna send back and get Willie Johnson. Just get out of my sight, get your stuff off the bandstand, get your stuff now. In the middle of the show! I takes my shit, excuse me, I takes my stuff, down, scared, trembling, just knowed I'm gonna get bopped any minute, and gets out of there. Sure enough, the chauffeur must have had an idea what was going on, he waiting on me, helped me put my amplifier in the trunk. Man, I cried a-a-a-all the way, just thinking that Wolf is going to get me. But he talked to me nice, man, he said go on, you're young, go on there, Muddy's a nice guy. But Muddy and that , it was a feud all the way through, 'cause they thought one could outdo the other one. They really was in a feud together, just like the McCoys, man! Then I got to playing with Muddy. Me and Otis Spann got together and went to playing his stuff. I had all Muddy's stuff down pat. Then Muddy tells me we was leaving town. Muddy say, we leaving town next week. I said thank you. That is all, then when I got to the job, that next Monday, we were fixing to leave town and he asked me, did I have enough clothes, I said, sure, I got enough clothes. I had me one suit, which he had had made, you understand. I had things to wear in the daytime, but I figured we wasn't gonna be gone that long . . .he said, man, that all you got, just one suit? I said, yeah, ain't this enough, we ain't gonna be gone that long. He said, we'll be gone about 40 days. So I'm thinking, what the, this man ain't told me nothing about no 40 days. He said, that's what we got. So I goes back and gets me some more clothes, bring my suitcase down, and then I hit the road with them.

Man, that forty days like to kill me. We had some of them jobs was a thousand miles apart, eight hundred miles – nothing under five hundred miles. I think about 20 days out of the 40 days that we had, didn't nobody get a chance to take a bath because by the time we got to another job, it was time to play. The last job, I'll never forget it, it was Miami, Florida, we got there 20 minutes before show time – I ain't seen guys put up equipment so fast in all my days. It took us 22 minutes to get everything up – we was two minutes late on that job, that is the only job out of 40 nights, man. And I had the haemorrhoids so bad I couldn't sit down. I couldn't even sit in the car, they bought me all these feather pillows that I had to sit on, all the way back to Chicago. When we got back to Chicago we had done 14 hundred miles, we got to drive all the way, well the guys did, I couldn't do no driving cause I couldn't sit down hardly, and we got to the 708 Club about an hour before show time – and we got to set up and play that same night! I called Wolf, man, I said I got the haemorrhoids, this guy done work me 40 days and 40 nights, I said I am quitting. You tell me you're ready to come back? I said that's it, I'll be there in three minutes. I'll be there in two minutes. And I went back to Wolf.

Raeburn Flerlage

Jimmy Reed, Trianon, Chicago

Howlin' Wolf and band with Hubert Sumlin on guitar, Sylvio's, Chicago 1960's

Chapter 7 – Notes

1: Eli Toscano was the proprietor of Cobra Records; Dixon brought both Buddy Guy and Otis Rush to the label

2: Lee Cooper also recorded some Blues material, including 'No Place To Go' with Howlin' Wolf in 1954

3: The Chicago Music Company at 18th and Halsted was an important factor in the local Blues scene – the city's best source for the latest equipment, it also reportedly offered good credit terms.

DOWN IN LOUISIANA

Trombonist Jim Robinson, drummer Dave Oxley,
Preservation Hall, New Orleans 1971

Clarence Gatemouth Brown takes one last look in the mirror to check his outfit. There's no need – it looks perfect: pristine cowboy boots, black jeans, rhinestone-studded Western shirt and a cool black Stetson. In an era where most people don't even dress up for dinner, Gatemouth Brown dresses up for breakfast, lunch, and afternoon tea.

Onward Brass Band at the Creole Parade, New Orleans 1973

The sun glints on the surface of Lake Pontchartrain as we drive through Clarence's home town of Slidell, Louisiana, which is just across the river from New Orleans. He nods to the odd acquaintance that we pass on the road, and provides a running commentary on points of interest – this place serves the best seafood in Slidell, this is his boat club, this is the store where he made his one and only arrest. Clarence is an honorary sheriff in the town – his police badge is lying between us on the bench seat, nestling next to his .38 revolver. Lucky, then, that he likes me. Even when I ask him the obvious question about his name. 'All it means is that when I was in class I could sing over the chorus and didn't need a microphone. I don't tell people about that any more, you're the first person I'm quoting that to for a long time.' I'd read some earlier interviews with Gate which had seemed to portray him as a tired, bitter man. Today was different – as he played the tape of his latest Verve album he whooped in excitement: 'listen to this, this lick here. This has got to be a Top Twenty Hit, man.' As we drive, he gives me the history of music according to Gate. It's a personalised view. T-Bone Walker, who inspired him to take up the electric guitar, was a sad man who played 'that depressing Mississippi stuff.' Guitar Slim, New Orleans' most famous guitarist was another loser – 'never used his head for nothing but a hat stand.' Freddie King, Otis Redding and English invasion groups also meet with his disdain, as does the music industry, and the soft-shell crabs we eat in a nearby restaurant. Such forthright opinions would count as boorish if held by someone with less charm than Brown, who merely wants to teach you the way the world works with minimal formality. Later in the evening he gives me an ad hoc driving lesson: 'You indicate when you go out of lane. That's good. But I noticed you didn't indicate a couple of times when you went back into lane. That's just as important.' I contritely promise to modify my road conduct, privately thinking that if my father were a Blues musician he'd probably be a lot like Gatemouth.

As evening closes in Gate takes me to his family house in Baton Rouge, proudly boasting 'People wouldn't believe a Blues singer could live in a house like this.' I don't mention that it's the small house on the bank of Lake Pontchartrain that makes me more envious, because if a maverick like Gate can make enough out of his music to buy a big house, the world's not as bad a place as the depressing shacks of Greenville might suggest. But as Brown puts it, Louisiana, compared to Mississippi, is a different country, and New Orleans is somewhere else again. According to Brown, his home state is simply superior to anywhere else in the world. It's easy to see why.

It's a fair generalisation to say that traditional Blues never really existed in the cultural melting pot of New Orleans – the city's rhythmic tradition meant that the music was almost instantly changed into rhythm and blues. The city's first great Blues guitarist, Lonnie Johnson, had more than a hint of the New Orleans dance heritage in his style, while Guitar Slim, originally a down-home Arkansas bluesman, once immersed in the New Orleans music scene made records that were as much R&B, Soul or Rock 'n' Roll as they were Blues. Outside the city, traditions changed, but the Louisiana Blues of Lightnin' Slim or Slim Harpo, or the Zydeco of Boozoo Chavis and Clifton Chenier were also marked by a rhythmic spriteliness – and an admirable individuality.

'I don't like just coming out with the same crap as everybody else,' reflects Clarence, lighting up another pipe of Brown's 'Special' Tobacco Blend. 'Like all

Roosevelt Sykes, wife Mercedes and family go fishing at Lake Pontchartrain near New Orleans

that stuff about how the audience is so beautiful. My audience ain't beautiful – they look like they come from another planet. And that's just what I tell 'em.' 'Don't you ever get embarrassed?' asks his daughter, 'what about that time you told me about when you were playing in Chicago and that bunch of kids were laughing at your clothes?'

'That was no problem,' he chuckled. 'I went straight up to them and asked 'What's the matter with you? Ain't you ever seen a cowboy before?'

Earl King:

My father died when I was a baby and I never got a chance to know him. It turned out that Tuts Washington was his best friend, and when I met Tuts and he found out who my daddy was he said, look boy, you sit down here and I'm gonna tell you all about him [1]. So he told me about how my father played piano down in the red light district. The piano players got work because they didn't have no juke boxes then, so every little place had a piano in it. That's what made New Orleans a piano town. They done had a lot of things, killings and all kinds of stuff in those places. My grandma used to tell me she used to be so afraid for my daddy, she said I'd stay up at night waiting for him, sometimes I used to

Moses 'Whisperin' ' Smith and his children, Baton Rouge Louisiana 1973

get my two dogs to go and get him, she said to me I'm not gonna go in them bars, but I go send my dogs in there and they find him for me. The red light district – everybody who talks about it will tell you about how it was really wild back them. And don't even mention in the war time when all the soldiers and sailors were coming into New Orleans, I was a kid then, I was just approaching my teens, and me and my friends used to go out and shine the sailors' shoes, and that was a wild time then, they be getting around everywhere.

So that's the reason New Orleans is known for pianos, because before the era of the jukebox all the little bars had a piano. Piano players would go in there and play by themselves. They used to call them honky tonks. Then when all the recording companies begin to came to New Orleans looking for talent, naturally a lot of the piano players would accompany the singers at auditions, and the best one that comes to mind for that is Huey Smith , and people like Professor Longhair – all those were known to play by themselves in the honky tonks.

They always say it was the piano players that brought about the sound of New Orleans, but that's not a fact, it was the drummers – the drummers changed the whole thing. All the record labels would say, we've come there to get the beat, the beat, they wouldn't talk about no piano players – it was the drummers. There were a lot of great drummers,

The Onward Brass Band at a New Orleans funeral 1972

Musicians' Union Club (now demolished), New Orleans 1971

drummers that really did something unique. In the early days when Earl Palmer was around, he played on every record you could mention, he probably doesn't remember all the ones he played on, from Little Richard to Fats, you name it. Then there was this guy called Charlie Williams – we called him Hungry – that was the one that turned the whole thing around. The Rhythm and Blues you hear today, it was Charlie that brought it about. He'd listened to Earl Palmer and all of those other drummers, and he took the traditional drumming, for traditional jazz, took those meters and added a kind of Latin touch to it, and that's the kind of rhythm you get today. Quite naturally, as in anything else there were drummers listening to him too, Smokey Johnson, Joe Monteles, Zigaboo from the Meters... it's like the painters, many painters start off trying to emulate others, and that's what happened to New Orleans. The other part of it is what we call the second line rhythm, which comes from the second line at the funerals – everybody learned how to play their own rhythms without even thinking about it. It's the rhythms that make this city's sound. Usually everyone figures it was the piano players, but it was the drummers that really did the trick.

Cosimo Matassa:

I try to explain New Orleans that by saying it was a dancing town. There were cultures in which music was a sit down and listen exercise, but in New Orleans it was a get up and dance exercise. So the whole aspect of how people played and what they played was different, and it created a lot of great percussion players because if you weren't any good, people quit hiring you. There is something about a tradition that develops people and attracts people with a natural bent to it, and that's what happened in the city, from Earl Palmer to James Blackwell, whose personality was odd, but his drumming was fantastic [2]. I can still remember his drum kit – it looked like something the Salvation Army threw away, half the buckles were missing and the rims that held the head down were warped, but he played absolutely marvellously – I get carried away thinking about it. Drummers were crucial, to the point that when they changed from using calf skins to plastic drum skins, it had a drastic effect on the recording process.

Tommy Ridgley:

New Orleans has always been a good town. You can talk about segregation, but here you can hardly segregate, because a lot of the time you didn't know the white people from the black people. You go downtown and you didn't know no black or white. I know more black people look like you who was at the dance Sunday night, and you would never believe they were black. The priest, I'm talking about the Catholic one, he had a lot of children downtown. Things was always different in New Orleans. And it's always been a pretty decent place.

Catman:

There were two major clubs in New Orleans, and that was the Dew Drop and the Tijuana. The Dew Drop was the up-market place – it had a nightclub atmosphere. People would dress. In fact there was a time Frank didn't allow you to enter unless you were dressed [3]. This was such a different era, in that era people dressed all the time, they were not wild, but they were a groovy crowd and they understood what was going on. Frank got the people automatically because they knew no matter who the stars were, they would be at the Dew Drop. Like BB King, he would play at the Blue Eagle then after the gig he would be jamming at the Dew Drop. The shows were terrific – it was all day and an all night thing, Friday, Saturday and Sunday, after that they would rest, but that weekend was terrifying, it was around the clock, it was a grind, there was no resting.

You started at twelve midnight, and you are supposed to get off at 4.30 really, but that never happened because the average musician got off from Bourbon Street and got there at two or three. The night's entertainment always consisted of a show. The show would start off with an MC, and he would be capable of doing jokes or singing, guys like Harold Batey or Tec Stephen. Then a shake dancer would be second, or else you'd have a tap dancer like Streamline Harris. After that the feature would come on, and there was always a fight who was gonna close the show. Maybe Joe Tex, Joe Turner, the big acts would come on at the end, but we would stay after the show was over, then the guys would come up and jam, and we would jam until 10 o'clock in the morning. The Dew Drop had no clocks inside, it was always dark at the front, so you don't really realise that it was daylight outside.

The place was famous for the female impersonators, we had a revue really, a regular revue. Patsy Valderre was the connoisseur, she was the boss of the female impersonators. Every Halloween was a big night, it was Patsy Valderre's night, they would bring out all the female impersonators from all over the city, all out of town, they would come and try and outdo each other with the dress and the hair and all these things.

The last show big show that they had, there was a guy named BB and BB could sing like Dinah Washington, I mean exactly – you stand outside that door and you would swear that was Dinah Washington. They would give prizes on that particular night. So gee, this was a great night for Patsy, you know these wigs, that people wear at Mardi Gras, all these different colours, and then you had some material that was like the wig, then he had a rug, a red rug, that he got from somewhere and a cab to bring him up in front of the Dew Drop – he comes out in front of the place and he had two guys that come and roll the rug out, like royalty, real royalty. The guy walks on the rug and he has this long gown on, and all this finery with his hair and all this stuff on the top, and he just know he's got it sowed up, that it's his night. But this guy BB, he goes down to see Virginia, Virginia Willis, this famous lady who would sew for everybody. She brought this BB to her house, sowed up a fine gown and loaned BB her fur coat, and BB came on the stage that night, and between the singing, the hair and the fine clothes, BB won the prize. And of course Patsy fell out for dead. I mean for dead. Patsy wanted to know what happened, said I got to win this prize, Frank said get up, you're making a show of yourself, and Patsy says she's gonna die, stretched out on that stage.

Clarence 'Gatemouth' Brown:

I was born in Vinton, Louisiana, that's right on the border of Texas. Right across the river is Orange Texas, and that's where I was raised. My dad played music at house parties for himself and for relaxation over the weekend and that's how I developed my skill in music, by playing along with him. My mom used to knock the furniture out of the living room, we always kept a big house, and kick all the furniture, move it back and that left room for everybody to dance. My dad played accordion, fiddle, mandolin, banjo and he sung French, he sung country and he sung bluegrass. My dad would sing real Cajun. Actually Zydeco was before Cajun. But the black man's version wasn't recognised until the white used some of the Zydeco to come up with that version of Cajun. But they are different music, you don't get Cajun and Zydeco mixed up because it depends on the instrument you're using; Cajun music is used with the fiddle, accordion, triangle and guitars, Zydeco is used with accordion, drums, bass and washboard. Now the Cajun music is a cross between French and Country, the Zydeco is a cross between Blues and French. Then the Texas music is different again, 'cause you have a lot of the Country and Big Band music, and over in New Orleans the music is based on the Caribbean, or Caribbean and Spanish, really. See, I'm a part of Louisiana, so I got this heritage and the Texas heritage, plus the world heritage.

Albert Collins:

What you gotta remember is that the Texas Blues, that's my kind of Blues, is a whole lot different from Chicago Blues or the anywhere else Blues for that matter. My particular sound came from hanging around the horn sections of big bands. When I was coming up it was T-Bone and Guitar Slim that were my inspiration on guitar – Gatemouth Brown was another big influence – and them big Texas Jazz bands.

I started out learning the piano, then when I made 21 I got a Hammond organ 'cause I wanted to sound like Jimmy McGriff, or my hero, Brother Jack McDuff. Anyway, there's this guy in a band who was gonna teach me how to play, and one night on my way over to him my car broke down on the highway and I had to leave it and the trailer on the

Albert Collins

Clifton Chenier

side of the road while I went to get the repair man. I come back and someone had stolen it! A 300lb organ and they just ripped it off! I never made that lesson and that was the end of Albert Collins the organ virtuoso. I had to find me something else fast and the guitar was the thing.

Boozoo Chavis:

I was born in 1930, and in the Twenties and the Thirties, that's when that Creole and the French music was out already. All of them older people, Joe Falcon and Nathan Abshire, who did 'Pine Grove Blues', and Ivor Lejeune, they was out there. I was a teenager, I was working in the rice field, and me and this young man called Elridge Davis, we would work together and then when it got to 12 o'clock we would practise. And then I listened to another man, a good friend of mine called Mr Lennie Pete. He was a very good musician. All of those hadn't cut no records. Then the other guys, they'd play some dances and they'd get me to play the house dance at the Rum Boat. They played the same music that the white folks were playing, the Cajuns. They just played it different. We played the 'Eunice' two step, and they played the 'Eunice' two step.

Lonnie Brooks:

All you could hear in Louisiana was Zydeco and Country and when we would hear Blues it was out of Nashville, the old Randy Record mart — we wouldn't get chance to hear the Blues except but twice a month. The Cajun music back then was like a branch off from Zydeco music, like Rock 'n' Roll is a branch off from the Blues — Zydeco was little more of a raw thing, a hand-me-down music. Clifton Chenier was the king. He started this stuff in Louisiana — a lot of people played accordion at that time because of him. This guy was making a thousand dollars a night back in the Fifties, back when people would only pay 50 cents to come in. When I talked to him about the music he was raised on, it was French music mostly — Cajun music and Zydeco music, but he could play Rock 'n' Roll and a lot of Fats Domino stuff. The thing about this music, is they've got a beat that no other music has and I mean it can make you just (clicks fingers) — as soon as you hear it you just want to get up and start bouncing around. That was one of the greatest things about it, because a lot of time people didn't know what they was singing, because some of the people didn't know how to speak French. But the beat was the main thing, that was the unique thing.

Tabby Thomas:

The music you get in New Orleans, everywhere else in Louisiana, it's all different. Back in the Fifties Baton Rouge was a small-town place. People say, man it must have been exciting, but it was just an every-day thing. You'd have Lightnin' Slim, Slim Harpo, Silas Hogan, Raful Neal, Whispering Smith playing at all these little cafés and clubs, I guess the club owners would pay them 40 or 50 dollars. There was something going on all the time, but it wasn't a big deal. It was JD Miller, Excello that had the big effect.

The first time I met JD Miller was on a Sunday morning, I went to his house, told him who I was, and said I came to see about making a record with you. He said come back at 10.30 and I'll record you, simple as that. He was ahead of his time — very experienced as far as the sound, and he'd get in there and work with you, make sure the guys were playing right, he was a good engineer — great. And I respected him and I still consider him as a good friend of mine, even though I didn't get no money from those esssions. But he gave me an opportunity to express myself on record, same as he did for a lot of other people. That inspired me to hustle a way forward playing for myself, and it gave me a background, a catalogue to work from.

Jay Miller:

I could list you a whole bunch of guys that I recorded – Slim Harpo, Lazy Lester, Silas Hogan, Lonesome Sundown. I never did go looking for anyone, that was a rarity – you got to keep in mind other than New Orleans, and New Orleans didn't fool with the real low-down blues, I was the only one did it, so they'd come over here – there was no other studios in the state but me and Cosimo. They call the stuff that I recorded Swamp Blues. Each area has their own type of Blues, Chicago, Memphis, it's all different. Louisiana Blues, that's just a little bit different again, it's a little more mournful. And I'm a big believer in percussion and that made us a little different than anyone else too, I used anything, Coke bottles, cardboard boxes, newspapers, walls – I even had a saddle I used as a sound effect. I'm crazy about Louisiana Blues myself – I like the low-down blues, and Lightnin' Slim was my big favourite.

I met Lightnin' more or less by accident. A coloured DJ by the name of Diggy Doo, he called me and said, Mr Miller, come over and listen to this band over here. To be honest with you the band wasn't much, I was about to walk out and when I was in the hall I hear a guy picking the Blues on a guitar, and I turned round and went back in. And it was Lightnin'. And I asked him if he did any singing. He said he did some. I said well, will you play the Blues for me, he played a thing, if it wasn't for bad luck I wouldn't have no luck at all, and I just went ape over that, so I had Diggy Doo bring him to Crowley. Now I needed a harmonica blower and a drummer, but I couldn't find either of 'em. I was told there was a good harmonica blower in Beaumont by the name of Wild Bill Phillips, so I got in my car and took off. Have you ever tried to find someone around the coloured area? Nobody had ever heard of him or anything. And I was on my way back to Crowley and I saw a cop, a white policeman on the corner. I stopped and told him who it was I was looking for and asked if he knew him, and where I could find him – I'd been looking for him for a couple of hours. He said yeah – we got him in jail. So we went over there, got him out, came to Crowley and recorded. But I still needed a drummer, and couldn't find one, so Diggy Doo, who never did any drumming in his life, I ask him, could you maybe keep time, he said I'll try, and we cut two sides on him and they were great.

What happened with the records was that I would lease them to Ernie Young, who had Excello Records, and you may not believe it but I was getting five and a half cents for 90% of records sold, and he didn't give me one cent for paying the musicians and doing the session. I wasn't getting much but it opened the door. I dealt with him quite a few years and finally got up to six and a half cents, which was still no money, and I didn't get any publishing money, and as I said we didn't even get to recover the money we spent. He was awfully tight. At that time I didn't know what was good and what was bad, I just wanted to get myself started.

Lightnin' was always my favourite Blues man. We went for many years after that until he borrowed a van from me, went to Baton Rouge and wrecked it, then he left and went to Pontiac, Michigan. Some of those boys made him believe I was gonna have him put back in the pen – he spent 10 years in the pen just for hopping a ride with some guys that

French Quarter, New Orleans

French Quarter, New Orleans

broke the law, he tells me he didn't have anything to do with it. But anyway, I never could get him back. I wasn't offended too much – I was thankful nobody got hurt, I had ample insurance and everything, but he was so scared 'cause I was personal friends with the governor. He was just scared to death. Two, three times I called him and I thought I had him coming back, and he changed his mind each time. Then one day I got a telephone call from Pontiac, his landlady called me, and said he had passed away. I asked her, how do you know my name? She said Lightnin' told me if ever anything happened to him to call me. He wasn't afraid of me personally, he was afraid of what he thought I might do. He was my friend and I believe I was his friend.

Chapter 8 - Notes

1:     Tuts Washington, born in 1907, was one of the first generation of New Orleans
       Blues-oriented piano players

2:     James Blackwell and Earl Palmer were two of New Orleans' premier session drummers

3:     Frank Pania was the owner of the Dew Drop Inn, Lasalle St, New Orleans – the city's leading
       nightclub. Catman is referring here to the city's nightclub scene around 1950

WHITE BOY BLUES

Keith Richards' Big E Levi's jean jacket is perfection in denim, precisely straddling that fine line between being nicely distressed and completely knackered. A bit like the man himself. Bizarrely, you find yourself wondering whether Keith employs a retinue of flunkies to wear-in his clothes for him – I know that it's the case with his beloved Telecasters, which Fender painstakingly make to authentic Fifties spec, then batter with hammers and burn with cigarettes. Here is a man worth a reported $50m, who spends a substantial amount of it on looking like a bum who makes his money playing bars at weekends. And ludicrous as it should seem, he pulls it off.

Rolling Stones Keith Richards and Charlie Watts backstage

Eddie Taylor, John Lee Hooker and Walter 'Shakey' Horton, Hammersmith Gaumont, London 1968

One of the musicians who played on Mick Jagger's last solo album spoke of the difficulties posed by addressing a legendary Rock aristocrat. He settled for calling him 'Mr Jagger'. There are no such quandaries with Richards – he's Keith, or Keef, through and through. Richards is a man without pretensions, who genuinely holds mentors like Chuck Berry or John Lee Hooker in the same esteem as The Rollling Stones. The first time I'd attempted to interview him was to talk about working with Hooker. Cold-calling his manager, instead of the usual brush off, I was told, 'if it's for John Lee, he'll probably do it.' Two days later, the man called me at home. Now, in his New York office, the same charisma, the same air of faint amazement that he's still around, are just as striking as they were on the phone. 'Yeah, when I first met guys like John Lee or Muddy, I really did believe they'd think we were prats,' he chuckles, lighting up another fag and sipping from the vodka and orange that has (temporarily) replaced his favourite bourbon. 'They're struggling to make a living out of music and along come these white boys, selling millions of records. I doubt whether I could have been as cool about it as they were, ha ha.' Keith is mildly surprised at being welcomed by his idols, surprised that The Stones made it through the Sixties with relatively little mayhem ('that guy died at Altamont... sometimes I can't believe it was just one, the way things were then'), surprised that they made money playing covers of Slim Harpo or Robert Johnson songs. The relatively obscure records by his musical heroes seem for him to be be divorced from the business he inhabits, from an age when music had mysterious and magical properties, before it opened up to the attention of the world's media. Although in the Nineties Richards' group doesn't attempt to craft pastiches of Thirties recordings, or cast themselves as authentic Bluesmen, Richards' whole attitude is evidence that without Jimmy Reed's shuffle rhythms, or Chuck Berry's two-note guitar lines, The Rolling Stones wouldn't even exist.

Billy Boy Arnold:

Let's put it like this: during the Thirties and Forties white people didn't hear our music. If they had, they would have bought Big Bill Broonzy, Sonny Boy, Arthur Big Boy Crudup and all those people too. Those artists would have been just as big as the guys are today if they had played them on the radio where white people could have heard them. But at that time anything that blacks did was sort of pushed down, but if they had heard Big Bill Broonzy, Memphis Minnie and all those guys, like they did Bo Diddley in the Fifties, they would have been major artists all over the world. It wasn't the record companies – it was Jim Crow, racism itself. Nobody consciously said don't listen to black music, it just wasn't promoted and they wasn't about to promote black music 'cause that would have been recognising the power that the black people had. Now my theory, my own personal theory, is that white people knew a lot about black people, they admired them and they saw the strength and the power that black people had and the soul we got. They browbeated blacks and used an economic strangle-hold on them because they were totally afraid and they felt totally inadequate – they were scared of what would happen if they really gave these people equal opportunities, or at least didn't block their progress. So it was more a fear thing. When I was a kid I could understand these type of things. I had my own theory of thinking of what it was, what racism was all about, and it was the fear of the black male. But I saw those barriers breaking down when I was on a tour with Johnny Guitar Watson and Fats Domino in 1957. We were all down in Louisiana and Texas, and Fats was drawing as many white people as blacks. They had a partition and the white kids had to be on this side and black kids were over here dancing and having a good time. The white kids could only look and they wanted to dance and enjoy the music – so they tore the partition down. The die-hard racists were saying, what the hell's happening? I knew then that things couldn't stay the same way they had always been.

John Mayall:

I started off listening to records because of my dad, really, we'd always have Jazz and Blues records playing around the house. Despite what you might hear, Blues records – and they would all be 78s – weren't too hard to find in England. At least we always seemed to have them around. I started off listening to Eddie Lang, Django Reinhardt and Lonnie Johnson, moving on to records by people like Josh White and Big Bill Broonzy.

I didn't even think about whether it was unusual for a white lad from Manchester to be listening to the Blues. With my first band, The Hounds Of Sound, we started off playing trad Jazz, then moved more into Blues, although maybe the audiences weren't too attuned to what we were doing. By then they were into Elvis Presley and Rock 'n' Roll, but as long as you played anything with a beat they were pretty happy. After the war there seemed to be a lot of kids who were getting into Jazz and Blues so what we were doing didn't seem outrageous. But anybody who was into the same music was a kind of soul mate. The first time we linked up with any kind of scene was when Alexis Korner and his Blues Syndicate played in Manchester. We opened up for him that night, and I got to talking to him, asking what it was like in London and so forth, so he was instrumental in encouraging me to come down to London and check it out. He introduced me to Rik Gunnell at the Flamingo and John Mansfield and Phil Hayward over at the Ricky Tick clubs which were just starting out. And that's how I got started.

Keith Richards:

It would have been around 1958 when I first cottoned on to John Lee Hooker, Muddy Waters and all of those other Chicago guys. I would have been around 15 or 16, I was at art school and records were passing around between aspiring guitar players and Bluesmen – bored 16 year old white kids. It was before I met Brian, it was even before Mick and I had got together musically... but I think it was the fact we were searching out these records that brought us together – we found out we weren't the only ones in the world listening to this type of music.

When I started playing all I wanted to do was play like Chuck Berry. I thought if I could do that I'd be the happiest man in the world, then when I found out I could do that I thought, maybe there is another aim in life. The idea of playing with Muddy Waters was 'when I get to heaven . . . if I make it there and he makes it there.' But I actually got to play with him, John Lee, Howlin' Wolf, Scotty Moore . . . I actually got to play with them all. You can't ask much more than that. And I got paid!

In 1962, starting a Blues band was not the way to stardom. It was aimed at giving people a kick in the teeth, spending a couple of years waving our Blues flags... then suddenly you're a pop star. You don't wanna be there but you are, and it's too late. The Sixties were so weird, especially if you were like The Beatles or ourselves, spending your life thinking, wouldn't it be great if this happened, or this. And then it did! Suddenly everything was going in line with what you'd fantasized, when you were lying around thinking, wouldn't it be great to stir it up a bit! But you didn't realise how big it was gonna get, you just wanted to shake them up a bit, not have any major revolutions or anything. What, you gonna have a revolution with a guitar? The other thing that made it all important was in fact the paranoia of the authorities. Not just in Britain, here too. These were bastions, nations and people the whole world relies upon to get fed – did they really spend their time listing us as a threat? This I can't believe. But it really happened. The other thing that

Chuck Berry about to go on stage at the Capital Radio Jazz Festival, Alexandra Palace, London 1979

scared the shit out of me was how incompetent they actually were! Their attempts at planting things, they'd find a little paper bag under the couch and go, gotcha! It was like a Monty Python sketch. I was brought up as a British schoolboy in the middle Fifties — and firmly believed Scotland Yard was incorruptible. Until I had to pay out ten grand and then get popped. And the scales fell from my eyes. But I know we weren't first. People like Robert Johnson, they've done it for us already. They didn't intend to, but they did.

The weirdest thing was that when we met Muddy he was painting Chess studios [1]. You walk in and start recording, on your hands and knees in this Mecca, and they say, you might like to meet this guy who's up on a step ladder in a white overall, and you say, who's that? That's Muddy Waters. It was another of those slaps around the face. His records weren't selling. And at the same time he was a real gentleman. I was sure he'd look down at us, but none of those guys were like that, or John Lee, it was like, we've had some babies, and they're white! And they sort of nurtured us. Those guys were gentleman, they saw wider than the music business. They immediately nurtured us, and had no reason to know that because they had in a year or two they'd be selling more records than they had in their lives before. I would have expected a 'get out of here white trash' reaction but those guys were bigger than that. Like John Lee, who just has a bigger heart, an inner vision of what's happening. John Lee is no spring chicken now, but I went over to his house for a barbecue just after a session, and he had a whole bunch of young ladies with him, all guitar players, so you end up in John Lee's front room with everybody plugged in hammering away and John just sits in the back there eating, going, yeah, that's pretty good. That gives you hope, that this guy's nearly twice as old as I am and he's still playing. When you start playing you don't realise what hurdles will come in the way. It's like looking over the edge — nobody's taken the music this far. It's a voyage of discovery. I'd be very happy to be 75 years old playing guitar and working on my stuff and having 15 girls all learning how to play guitar from me.

Sam Lay:

I was playing in a Chicago joint called the Blue Flame, which is no longer there now, it's an empty field out there. It would be around 1963, I was playing with Little Smokey Smothers, and one night this fellow came in and Smokey said, hey man. He said we're gonna call this white boy and let him play some harmonica, and he called him up, I didn't even remember his name at first, he came up and played and the next weekend he played again. I noticed then that that is when the whites would come from the North Side to the South Side to get a chance to see Paul Butterfield, and they started to make a little bit of money out of it, and it kinda took off from there. Okay, over here with Little Smokey, we were making, top money, seven dollars a night. I would catch Little Smokey most of the time, when I wasn't busy with Wolf. With Wolf we were playing at a place called Sylvio's on Lake Street, and we were making, I believe, 12 dollars and 50 cents. The only thing that took Butterfield to get me away from Wolf, he came and asked me, if we could put a band together I could make a little more money and we could work more nights steady. I said steady for what, he said, we could work four nights a week right here in town and I know a place where we could get $20 apiece a night. That's a long ways from 12. I said let's do it. He had talked about getting Little Smokey but instead he got Elvin Bishop. So I left right away, and the first weekend we played, hey that was $80, and we worked four nights a week. Eighty bucks is a long ways from 12 — and we worked like that for quite a while. That was more than I ever made playing in my life, 'cause on the

Raeburn Flerlage

Otis Rush and band playing Peppers Lounge, 43rd Street, Chicago with Paul Butterfield and Mike Bloomfield in the audience

road with Wolf out of town we would get $22 and 50 cents, and in most cases we had to pay our hotel bill out of it. So it was the $20 a night that was the reason for leaving. I got greedy for money!

I think the first time I was made aware of the people in Europe was playing Blues, Howlin' Wolf went on a programme called *Shindig*. The Rolling Stones had mentioned him, something to that effect, and they played one of Howlin' Wolf's songs, it didn't sound like Wolf but it was Wolf's song, and it was Blues. That was when I started being wired up of what was happening. I was glad of it because, I said, maybe it will open a door for us.

With Butterfield we went to playing for white crowds at Big John's on Wells in the North Side [2]. And the way I felt was, the way people treated us over there, if heaven is like this, then I better get ready to go to heaven playing Blues — people treat you good, we'd get everything we want, folks were friendly, we met different people every night, and I kinda got spoilt. Now they're the only places I like to play. I got some good audiences here in the country — but there's no audiences like the audiences in Europe. They really treat you like Kings in Europe. Beautiful people. I only been one time and I been trying to get back ever since.

There were guys on the South Side thought I shouldn't be playing on the North Side. They resented it, a few of them — maybe they thought I was thinking I was better then them. But the guys in the band, right away I tell you Butterfield or Elvin Bishop, neither one of those guys never showed me any sign of prejudice. No signs. Wherever they were coming from, they were coming with me, because I was with them. They appreciated me, and I appreciated them. Elvin will tell you today, I taught Elvin a lot of stuff on the guitar, old traditional Blues and stuff, and there's some words to some of the songs I had to teach Butterfield because he couldn't make them out from the records. I feel good about the stuff we did together.

I did the first album with Butterfield, and there was the stuff we did with Dylan, like Newport and Highway 61. We all got on great, just musicians making music and having a good time. The last time Dylan was in town I went by his hotel to drop off some photos for him, and I left them at his box, 'cause I had to get back to work, then when I got back to work he called me and we're on the phone for 30 minutes, and everybody on the job went ape. It was amazing to me because everybody on my job is black, what would they know about Bob Dylan, but they did. They all looked at me like as if I was crazy, like I was supposed to fly away or something. But those people, just like Sly and the Family Stone, they are everyday people. But sometimes I sit back and it comes across my mind, time couldn't be gone by this quick – I still picture myself slipping off from the campus from my elementary school down to the corner to play 'Juke' on the juke box by Little Walter, and I wind up here.

Jimmie Vaughan:

I learned to play from the radio. The first song I learnt was 'Honky Tonk', by Bill Doggett, and I learned to play my own, weird, version of that. Then I started finding out about BB King and everything, then this guy told me about Little Walter and Muddy Waters, and it went on from there. There's something about that music – it stays with you forever. There's one Jimmy Reed album – any album, it doesn't even matter which – I will never get tired of it. I can play it all day long, over and over – it doesn't get old, and I've been playing it since I was 14. It was through music that Stevie and I communicated, through playing – we did it so much when we were kids it was sort of second nature to us. I was the older guy and I played before Stevie, so he learned by watching me learn, then I split, then the next time I saw him he was amazing.

It was really Freddie King who taught me about being professional. I played with him for quite a time, and it was very scary. He would play these incredible solos, had this huge Dual Showman amp, and he was a big man, a very powerful, commanding guy, and he'd play all this stuff, then he would look around and point at you! I had this little bitty amp and I felt like a little kid. And I was. But he was very nice. He controlled the situation – not in a mean way, it was just that he knew what to do. He was teaching me. He gave me the feeling he thought I was OK, that he liked the way I played. One time he came to my gig in Dallas, came in for a drink with some friends, and I was on a break so he said, c'mon get in my car, so we were driving around town and he was playing me Robert Johnson, and Jimmy Rogers and all this stuff in his Cadillac. And he'd do stuff on stage, like he'd say, don't do that any more, do this, and then he'd show me something. He was like a big brother, a coach or something. I think he wanted to know that there were people who were trying to do what he was doing. He was trying to pass something on.

Joe Louis Walker:

I grew up in the Fillmore district in San Francisco – we had the Fillmore Auditorium before Bill Graham got there, and we'd go and see James Brown, The Temptations, Bobby

Fred McDowell at the Bridgehouse, Elephant and Castle, London 1969

Bland. I used to open up for all the old guys coming to the city 'cause I was one of the few young Blues guys there. Everybody from Lightning Hopkins, Fred McDowell, Earl Hooker – I played with him for a while – Freddie King, Magic Sam, Muddy Waters, Howlin' Wolf. My mother and father were Blues fanatics, so I listened by osmosis. Then growing up, everybody start playing that music, and I could play it naturally – guys would do 'Little Red Rooster' by The Stones, I would do the Howlin' Wolf version!

The San Francisco scene happened 'cause all the Chicago players, a lot of white Chicago players, even some black ones, moved out there – Luther Tucker, Mike Bloomfield, Charlie Musselwhite who was about the first – they all moved out and it changed the whole complexion of the music scene. What you had before was basically the psychedelic guys trying to play Blues – The Grateful Dead, trying to do 'Good Morning Little Schoolgirl' – then the real guys started coming out, the Paul Butterfield guys, then Bloomfield started bringing out the old black guys, Carey Bell, and he campaigned for BB to play for the first time at the Winterland, and it started giving people an idea of what the real thing was. I shared an apartment with Bloomfield for a while and we used to stay up all night talking music. Then the Matrix opened up, a little club where I used to play, and you'd have Mississippi Fred and Magic Sam, I saw Magic Sam's debut there, six people in the club, and I musta brought half of those with me, but the next night he played at the Winterland with John Mayall and there's two, three thousand people. They'd come to see John Mayall, and here's Magic Sam. And the people loved Sam. That was indicative of how the music business works. It impressed on my mind, same as it is today, it gives you a realistic view – like if BB King does an album it's just great, but if BB King does an album with U2 it's humungous. That's the way of the music business.

What happens, and this is always the case, if you get a Rock guy, and he hires a Buddy Guy, or a BB King or an Albert Collins, what they bring is credibility. It doesn't make any difference what song the white guy does, he could have been playing heavy metal two days before, but if he gets one of these Blues guys, whose been playing Blues all their life, on his record, it virtually co-signs for his credibility. The Blues musician then gets a little higher visibility, and they sell a few more records. But in every instance it's been to the Rock guy's advantage. And I'm not saying there's a right or wrong to it, just saying that that's the facts, and it's always been like that, back as far as the London sessions with Muddy and Wolf playing with the guys over here. And I know for a fact it helped with the Rock guys' credibility, as far as playing Blues.

In San Francisco it was Albert King and Freddie King who really benefited. They were the chosen two, the recipients of all the adulation and accolades. Muddy never really catered for that new audience. But all those Blues guys who played there were happy, 'cause they were making money for once. I didn't know Albert back then but I used to play Freddie's guitar. The guy was so into music, he was a guitar fanatic, and it didn't make any difference who or where or how, he just loved to play. And when he hooked up with Shelter, Leon Russell, it was a perfect match for him [3].

Taking drugs was the one bonding thing for everybody, all the musicians, at the time. Everybody dibbled and dabbled. The only person I ever saw who didn't take drugs at that time was Frank Zappa – he'd fire guys if they smoked weed and stuff. One time, when John Mayall came to the States and Mick Taylor was playing with him – I got to know Mick real well, 'cause of Bloomfield. They were playing at the Avalon Ballroom that night, Mayall's band, Muddy's band and Big Mama Thornton. Later on we got on stage, me and a bunch of local musicians, and everybody was high as a kite, and we literally . . .everybody was playing in different keys and nobody knew, is this a shuffle or what, and we

Dezo Hoffman / Rex Features Ltd

John Mayall

Muddy Waters (centre) and Brownie McGhee (right) backstage at Fairfield Hall, Croydon England 1964

trashed the show. Now all of those people were strict band leaders. So at the end of the night, the Avalon had a small dressing room, and Muddy had his band in one corner, John Mayall had his band in one corner, and Big Mama Thornton had her band in the other corner. And they were all just cursing the bands out. It was so funny. Three generations of players in this one little room, and all of them were getting cussed out.

Chapter 9 - Notes

1:    The Rolling Stones recorded at Chess studios in 1964, during their first US tour

2:    North Side audiences were almost exclusively white, as opposed to the almost exclusively black audiences of the West Side and South Side clubs

3:    Freddie King, who had previously recorded for Federal/ King, recorded more Rock-oriented material for Cotillion in 1969, and Leon Russell's Shelter label in 1970

Buddy Guy outside Theresa's, Chicago 1972

IF IT WASN'T FOR BAD LUCK

Hotel rooms this small just aren't supposed to exist outside of down-town Tokyo. There's a maximum of two feet of space around the double bed, just enough for Buddy Guy to fit his Guild guitar and a couple of suitcases. Buddy is blurred with jet-lag, and the stuffy, fetid atmosphere of one of Kensington's less classy hotels doesn't help. Over the next couple of hours he tells me his life story as if it's a dream from which he hasn't quite woken. There's a stream of stories, of inspiring collaborations with Willie Dixon or Howlin' Wolf, or of grinding toil, driving trucks in Chicago blizzards. It's 1987, he's had no major label releases in the last decade, and it looks as if the future could contain more in the way of drudgery than it does inspiration. 'No,' I tell him, 'the kids are coming out to see you again. There's going to be more people getting into real music, played by real people again. You'll see.' After watching him that night, still fiery, still inspirational, I thought that maybe it wasn't just bluster – that Guy and the other musicians like him who'd dropped out of favour throughout the Seventies and Eighties might just find an audience once again.

Cotton Fields, Mississippi Delta

Guy and his contemporaries have no monopoly on hardship – there are just as many sad tales of white Rock 'n' Roll musicians who enjoyed fleeting fame without the attendant riches, or British invasion groups whose two per cent royalties disappeared into the black holes of off-shore bank accounts, never to be seen again. Few of those musicians, however, could still put on a show like Buddy Guy, Albert Collins, or Jr Wells – Blues players who saw their black audience fade away in the mid Sixties, with their new-found white audience following a decade later. It would take the advent of new specialist independent record companies and the concept of niche marketing to engineer a revival – for a select few artists. By 1995 Guy had enjoyed his third chart album – but the queue of similarly inspiring performers waiting for a taste of similar success is a long one.

Robert Ward:

You think you know about catching hell, you know that other people did it, but you never think it would happen to you. But I found out about it. I found out about catching hell.

The stuff I done to make a living, man, let me name it. Pump wood, lumber stacking, saw mill, laying concrete in the street, bricks, rocks, mixing cement, like to kill myself, I did a little bit of everything, and I did a lot a lot of truck driving, with North American Van line, worked for them a while too. I had to give up music, my first wife died, I had six little children to look after. I didn't really give up playing, I just couldn't be in public. I was too busy trying to survive and make a living for them. Man I caught so much, even went to prison trying to survive, went for two years but didn't do but one.

This is how it happened. I was trying to feed the kids, I didn't have nothing in the house. So I went out one night, I didn't have no flour, no rice, no beans, no nothing...plus I'd just buried my wife and my momma, they died a year apart from each other, my momma in Georgia, my wife in Ohio, and they both died around Mother's Day a year apart, so all that was killing me. And then I moved my family down to my mom's house, 'cause we owned that there, a nice little place, then I went back to Ohio to get my children and a few things. All I owned was a Lincoln and a U-Haul home. After we buried her we left my momma's place nice, I could have lived there, I could have made it. But when I got back there wasn't no rug on the floor, no furniture in there, no nothing. That's the truth. I put the key in the door opened it, and there wasn't nothing left. I just sit down with the kids and cried. So that's hardship. So then I had to do something, but by me being from Georgia, down in the country where people mentally deaf, dumb and blind and they's going, Robert Ward, bigtime with the Ohio Players, I know he got money, he got a white Lincoln! Yeah, they looking at materialistic this and that and yet I'm about to die from starvation. So I went out looking for something, and this place was closed, this club where I used to go play. I was hoping somebody was playing there so I could maybe get a few coins or something. And then the door was opened, I didn't know if someone left it or not, I just touched it and it come open easy , and I went in. And there was some stuff sitting there, all kinds of stuff! Cooler full of beer, and liquor, and I looked out, opened a few of them, and I left it there. But they had some equipment there, and I got a few of them, put it in my car and went home. Put it up on the bed, wait until the next day 'cause it were late, I'm gonna sell it and buy some food, feed me and the kid's gonna eat. So then they came, the authorities came. I'm just sitting there on the bed teaching my two boys the bass and one of my kids he says, daddy look at all them lights round the house! Look at all that! And I'm going what? Yeah, they got me. Course, somebody had seen Robert Ward and his big white Lincoln, and it stuck out like a sore thumb. You can imagine, it stuck out like a sore thumb! So I showed 'em the empty cupboard, there's nothing in

Otis Rush, Chicago 1971

Otis Rush and daughter, Chicago 1971

there, and they said, yeah, we would have did it too, any man would have, but we got to do our job. So I said, yeah, I can understand that.

Otis Rush:

The time I was with Cobra they wasn't doing too much for me but at least they was releasing the records. That's more than I can say for the rest of the companies. I didn't know when I was doing good! After Cobra I went with Chess – two years I signed the contract for, we recorded a lot of tracks, and I got one record out over the two years. Two sides in two years. Then after two years, when I leave them I went with Duke, Don Robey out of Houston Texas, signed for five years, waited and looked at the walls for five years and I had one record, so that turned me out that way and I had bad luck ever since.

I remember I was in the 1815 Club, and they called the guy who ran it Boss. I'm sitting down there talking to Boss in the intermission – Magic Sam had just died, Boss used to manage him, he'd played in his club, and he wanted to take me and book me like he did Sam. So I said, yeah – this might be my opportunity, you know, some lose, some win, and Sam lost. Maybe my luck was going to turn at last. So we spent some time talking, and then I went on stage. We was playing when there was a big commotion over in the corner, then another over here, in front of the stage, and I'm thinking what's going on – it was a war, all these people fighting. Now Boss is over there and there's these two ladies who worked at the County Hospital in Chicago, and they had these scalpels, surgeons' knives, little sharp ones, and I see them hitting him, pecking at him, one in behind of him, and one in front hitting him up here in the chest. Now he's hitting them back, I saw heels go up in the air, you can see panty hoses, and he knocked 'em across the table with all the drinks flying. Man, he knocked 'em all out, but he musta started bleeding within from the surgeon's knife. He just – his head just slumped over and he died right there in front of the stage. I musta seen four or five people get killed in Chicago clubs. Another time a guy on 44th and Wentworth got shot with an army rifle. We're playing on stage and suddenly I'm thinking, oh my God, and there's a hole over here, right behind me. And the guy's down here in front of me. I'm trying to get out of the door but it's crowded, but that bullet musta hit him so hard it just flipped him over. His foot was where his butt was sitting, hanging up on the stool like he just turned a flip. I thought, I'm out of here, got my guitar and left my amp and had to wait a long time before I got that amp back. It was shaky. But I survived – I was lucky, that time. Lucky and unlucky.

I signed to Capitol Records around 1970. It was a big label, and I figured they'd be able to do me some good. At last I'm thinking, I'm on a big label, that's what I need, I'm reaching for my goal, and it just didn't work. My bad luck hit me again. From '71 to '76 or '77 I'm waiting for that record to come out, but they didn't want the record, they didn't want to fool with it [1]. Behind all this, all the hesitation and the years in between making albums I went to quit. That's why I didn't go in a studio. Occasionally, I was working out of New York at Tramps – there was this guy who helped me out and they liked me there, so I could go there three or four times a year. Someone else might phone me for a special engagement. The other nights I was shooting pool, trying to rip off other people.

Dave Myers:

Chess – how do you think he got rich? I done lived it, pal. I might not say it the way you can understand it. How do you think he got rich? Chess, see – the main thing out there is control values. Once you got something you can control that everybody needs, you can utilise it. See I can explain from the nitty gritty, I can run it from the very beginning to you. Oh yeah, Chess got rich. You know how he got rich? Shit, when he's collected Muddy Waters, here was a man can hardly write his name. Now I don't have to tell you any more about that do I – do I have to explain all that to you? You know he's gonna get wasted. And when you find a dumb sonofabitch like me, with the knowledge you have, technically, is a lot of curves you can throw on my ass. That's why I made the example, I said Muddy can't even write his name. Boom. The whole answer comes right there. By him not being knowledgeable enough to understand contracts, political things, technical things he needs to know, he didn't have a chance man.

I'm not suffering. I'm not suffering shit. I took care of myself and I looked at things and figured it out for myself so it wouldn't destroy my mind like it did my brother. Peoples like Earl Hooker, all those great musicians, they was well groomed people, here comes a guy from nowhere makes all the money... and they couldn't take it. And you wear your mind down and that body's gone. I know all this shit. I'm doing OK, I don't have to worry – look over there, that's my car, paid for, I don't owe shit on it. I took different directions to make it possible for myself so I didn't have to eat shit, man. You get tired of eating shit. But those kids eat shit, and that's what killed them. So I understand that, sometime I get

Lunchtime card session at Mrs Moore's Paradise Lounge,
Mound Bayou Mississippi 1974

The 'H&H', Capricorn Records' local restaurant, Macon Georgia

a little crazy thinking about it, how come this shit happens. Man, it's a bother what's going on out there. The ones that get the money and can get the support, those are the ones that are gonna make it. You can't stop it, I ain't talking about stopping it, and I don't resent it, but I like what's right about anything. I like the right thing, and I give that to any human being, I never been a prejudiced man in any direction, 'cause all peoples has they rights. I know these things. Whatever you do I want you to get the benefit of what you did, I don't want no motherfucker to come from nowhere and steal your shit.

Willie Kent:

Oh well, hard times, working with any band, if you're trying to run a band, is you go out and you work, and then when you get through working, and the guy say well, I didn't make no money. Now everybody's sitting around waiting on you, waiting to get paid. So you pay them – see when I started playing, what was you making eight, ten dollars a night, if you made 15, oh man you were doing good, if you made 20 you was in business. Those was hard times, 'cause you had to pay them whatever happens. Then a lot of times you go different places, and when you get there they cancel the job on you. You use your last money almost to get to work, and then you got to try to come back. And everybody's looking at you to get paid. I was a truck driver, so I would drive trucks and play at night, and I would save my vacation time 'cause if we got ready to go someplace I would always

Just off Highway 61, Shaw Mississippi 1976

Elm City North Carolina 1973

have time up. I worked 12 years without a vacation, and the majority of the time, if we went some place, Florida or some place like that, it was over a weekend and I would be back that Monday and go right back to work Tuesday. I was working like 12 and 14 hours a day. And then a lot of jobs you'd play was 4 o'clock places, and I would get off at four and have to be at work at six thirty or six. That was rough. And have to stay awake and drive all day too. Then when it's hot, the cab of a truck is twice as hot as it is on the outside, there was no air in the truck, it be cool when you're going, but when you're stopped or stuck in traffic, man it be hot. We had on average most of the time 150 miles radius, or 200 miles, then you would drive there, pick up your load, and a lot of the time when you have a small truck you'd have to load it and unload it yourself. And that was hard work because I was hauling like scrap metal, and scrap metal you have drums that weigh twelve or fourteen hundred pounds. And one man handling it up. It was hard work, real hard work, 'cause you load the truck and then have to drive it too. So I did that, I worked for a guy called Don Ross about 21 years. It was a small company, wasn't that many of us worked there, it was like a family — it was nice.

What happened was, I started getting sick and I was kind of tired — I'd get tired real easy. I didn't know what was wrong, so I went to the doctors, and the doctors run me around for I don't know how long, two or three years, or longer than that. Really seven years, telling me that this was wrong, that was wrong, they told me I had everything, but it

House of the blues, Palmetto Georgia 1978

Billy Goodman busking, 42nd Street subway station, New York

turned out I had a blockage. Fortunately I didn't have a heart attack, and if I'd have had one it would have killed me. It happened one day, when three times I had to stop and rest, finally I go see the doctor to see what's going on, then they found out that I had a blockage. I had to have a heart bypass, three heart bypasses. If they had of found out what it was seven years before when I told them, before it maybe got so serious, I wouldn't have had to have any surgery.

When I came out of it, I came out owing about 30-some thousand dollars. The whole thing was 47,000, the insurance picked up part, and I ended up owing 18,000. Then you got other bills and things, and you're not able to work. Along that period I almost lost my home and everything else 'cause I got behind, couldn't pay my bills, and couldn't draw my workers compensation 'cause I wasn't able to work. My wife was working but she wasn't making enough money to take care of everything. Boy, that was rough times. About three weeks after I was out of hospital, I ended up going back to work playing. I wasn't able to stand up all night 'cause the weight of the guitar was too much. Then I messed up one of the valves that they did, by lifting something I wasn't supposed to. They started to collapse and I had to go back in the hospital. I wondered how long I would last or would I be able to play, but after about four months the doctor told me I could go back to work on the trucks. But by now I'd decided, I'm not gonna go back to work on the truck no more. I'm just gonna leave it alone, 'cause my kids was of age, and I ain't gonna go back. I'm gonna do what I wanna do, and that's play and sing. Fortunately, when I started putting in more time playing things, started getting a little better. By now I'd already started picking up a little bit of recognition here and there, and by devoting more time to it, it worked better.

I don't know why I have to go on with this, I guess it's just a feeling, liking what you do. I guess like everybody else, I want to put some songs together that after I've done gone on or whatever, somebody else will pick up. Just like people started doing some of Howlin' Wolf's songs, or Muddy Waters' songs or Elmore James' songs. You want to leave something, that somebody will say well, you know, you were here, and at least you did something out of your life. I don't want to live and don't do nothing. I want to leave something. Something people can remember. Maybe some young musicians can come along that say, Willie Kent did that, I'm gonna see if I can turn it round and do something with it. Something like that.

Johnny Guitar Watson:

You know when I think back about how I was robbed, it's just sickening, man. However, that was then and this is now. In the old days I didn't know any about administration, it wasn't important, I would have paid to record at that point. Modern Records were OK, man, they just didn't care anything about me, when they got BB, they didn't care about nobody else. Seemed like I had that kind of luck 'bout everywhere I went, I get to King and they get James, and I'm thinking man, what is this, everywhere I go someone shows up [2]. I had a hard, terrible time through all those years not having records and trying to survive. And that's the way it went until I met Mike Vernon and he introduced me to Dick James [3]. I didn't have any success in all those years man then I got the Grammy nomination as the best new vocalist at the age of 30 I'm saying to myself this a joke? But better late than never is what I always say.

Mike Vernon got my number, I don't know how, but he's a big Blues fan, and he called me and said, there's this guy in England you need to meet. Well, over here they wouldn't give me $5000 for nothing, but Mike tells me this guy has had a big misunderstanding with Elton John and is looking to start a new label. I found out later they didn't really expect a big success, it was possibly a tax write off, and they didn't really expect anything big to happen. Dick said Mike speaks very highly of you, and I had some stuff I already did, demos of a couple of songs – Dick basically said go ahead and do what you want to do.

Man, when I recorded that album I had a serious ego problem, and I felt like I could do anything – and somehow it all worked, it was the strangest thing. I was having all these arguments with these people who were supposed to know how to make records, who were telling me, you're crazy man. But it all worked, they made a tremendous amount of money – and we did OK.

Today I'd be too terrified to even try and make an album the way I made that one. I did all the horns on studio time, said to the musicians, bring your manuscript and your horn and play what you want when you get there! Then when I told the promotion people what the title of the album was they were going, Jeez, this man is crazy. We can't get that on the radio. But Dick was great, said if that's what Mr Watson wants, that's what we'll do! I'm so happy he was that confident – the album wouldn't have happened if it wasn't called 'Ain't That A Bitch'. Then I had the idea of matching the sleeve to the artwork, which is why we had the dogs on the sleeve. Then when I wanted to do 'A Real Mother',

Bill Greensmith

Johnny 'Guitar' Watson, Los Angeles 1974

I had my real mother, pushing me in a Seville baby carriage, and it worked – in fact we got an award for that one. Then 'Funk Beyond The Call Of Duty', with the tank with Cadillac hubcaps, ha ha ha ha! Boy, I was having so much fun. People were saying this guy Johnny Guitar Watson is out of his mind! But I was just having so much fun and I was a little mad too, I really was. I went all the way. Whatever direction I saw something going, I just went all the way.

And during the Seventies I was in limos everywhere I went. Did we have wild times? Are you kidding? At that time, everybody was doing drugs, even myself. I didn't escape, nobody escaped, it was just a part of that time. Everybody was snorting cocaine, smoking weed, and man you're talking about wild, it was just... wheeeeeeee I can't even begin to tell you how it was. Looking back now on that time, it's frightening – it's such a dangerous way to go about things, I'm just thankful to God I even made it through that period and still have my sanity. That's exactly what that was about, it was just incredibly wild. That's what it is, man. I don't know anyone that escaped, anyone that says they did was a liar. Snorting drugs was just as normal as drinking a coke. And the managers contributed to it a lot of the time – that is absolutely a fact, man. It was new, very easy, and a lot of the guys became prostitutes for that kind of lifestyle. Then as time went on, some made it and some didn't – it took its toll for sure. Like Sly, he didn't make it out, and he was one of very many that didn't [4]. It required a lot of discipline and a lot of strength to stop doing it, to leave it alone and change your life around, and it wasn't the easiest thing to do. And I can only speak for myself man, I thank God I was able to stop and not blow myself away.

Chapter 10 - Notes

1:   Rush, along with Mississippi Fred McDowell and Lonnie Brooks, signed to Capitol Records in 1969/70. Capitol were hoping for crossover success with the three bluesmen, but after poor sales for Hurt and Brooks, refused to release Rush's already-recorded album. It was finally released on the Bullfrog label in 1976, ironically titled 'Right Place, Wrong Time'

2:   When Watson recorded for Modern, BB King was the label's biggest artist – similarly, Watson's tenure at Federal/King was overshadowed by James Brown

3:   Mike Vernon was the UK's best-known Blues producer of the Sixties, responsible for ground breaking albums by the likes of the Bluesbreakers and Fleetwood Mac. More recently, he founded the Blues-oriented Indigo and Code Blue labels. Dick James, previously Elton John's manager, owned the DJM label, home of Watson's million-selling 'Ain't That A Bitch' album

4:   Sly: Sly Stone

BLUES IS HERE TO STAY

When I walked out of Holly Springs' video store a little old white-haired lady was waiting for me. She'd heard me asking for directions to Ackie Pro's record shop. 'I just wanted to tell you,' she whispered, 'that place is in the bad part of town. We don't normally go there.' She turned tail before I thought to ask what fate she thought might befall me, but I was struck by the subtlety of her geography: all I had to do to get to Ackie's was cross the street.

As I crossed that crucial thoroughfare and walked up to Ackie's for a rendezvous with Jr Kimbrough, it became obvious that both Ackie and Jr occupy an invisible America. Ackie's shop isn't in the Holly Springs phone book, and none of the whites I spoke to knew of its existence, despite the fact that it's just 20 paces off the main street. Kimbrough, a musician celebrated in the pages of *Rolling Stone* magazine, and whose juke joint is discussed in tones of awed reverence by the growing number of Blues fans who've made the pilgrimage, is similarly invisible in his home town – from across the street, at least.

Roosevelt 'Booba' Barnes outside his own Playboy Club, Greenville Mississippi 1988

146

Roosevelt 'Booba' Barnes, inside the Playboy Club, Greenville Mississippi 1988

David Kimbrough himself is about 65 years old, walks with the aid of a stick, worked full time as a farmer until relatively recently, and has lived in this small town for most of his life. He's a country Bluesman, the stuff of public service documentaries, of university research, of worthy criticism. But that evening, when performing in his garishly-painted juke joint, Kimbrough, who has mastered the impossible art of simply playing what he feels, demonstrates that this music can still be as gloriously subversive as anything ever produced by a music industry which delights in calling itself alternative. Kimbrough comes from the same state and culture as the likes of Charley Patton or Willie Dixon, so we call him a Bluesman, even though his music boasts inexplicable parallels with psychedelia, or Neil Young, or Spacemen Three. His music is not traditional – it is iconoclastic, as was the music of his forebears such as Blind Willie Johnson, Lightning Hopkins, or John Lee Hooker. At a time when Blues music should surely be just another product, predictable fodder for the advertising or music industries, Kimbrough represents a future which is gloriously unassimilated. Ninety years from when the Blues was first noticed, this music still retains its potential to be refreshingly direct, yet disturbingly outlandish.

Booba Barnes:

Don't believe what they is saying about the Blues not being around. The Blues is still around. I'm still around. I learned from Howlin' Wolf, I was lucky enough to sit in with him when I was just a kid, and now I'm doing what he used to go. Carrying it on. When people come and watch me they're gonna find out what they're missing. I'm gonna give 'em the best time they ever had. Mississippi Delta Blues is still living, you got people like RL Burnside, Jr Kimbrough, Big Jack Johnson, they're all still playing that music, and they still get people in. Up here in Chicago you get the whites like the music more, but down in Mississippi you still get the blacks that always listened to it. My club, you get some whites coming in there, but it's mostly blacks that support it. This is real music. My songs come from the heart. I think about things and I write. I give it all I got – I let it all come out. I don't hold it back. That sort of music ain't ever gonna go out of fashion.

Robert Cray:

We all came to the Blues in different ways. When I first picked up a guitar back in 1965, I wanted one because of the Beatles. It wasn't until a few years later, when my high school band broke up, that a friend and I started listening to Buddy Guy and BB King, Elmore James and Magic Sam, and I realised, we've got all of these records at my mom's house! So I started stealing those records, and learning those licks off them. It was seeing Albert Collins in 1969 that made me realise how powerful the music could be.

People ask if I see myself as a Blues singer, and I do, but a lot of the pigeonholes that we use don't get us anywhere. I'm caught between being a Blues man and a Soul man, but it's not as if there has to be this big dividing line – look at Little Milton Campbell, he's got the uptown R&B thing going, and he can tear down the place playing Blues. I don't think you can go back and isolate the Blues from the music that came after it, or ignore the effects of Jimi Hendrix and people like that. For a generation like mine, there are too many other influences to make a distinction between Blues and whatever else. That's not to say that Howlin' Wolf wasn't influenced by other forms of music too, but he came from the Delta, and we're in a different day and age now. But we're lucky to have some

147

Robert Cray

gentlemen still playing, guys in their late fifties or sixties, who learned from the originals. If people are starting to rediscover players like John Lee Hooker, or records by Albert Collins or Hubert Sumlin, that's got to be a good thing. The fact that people like John Lee Hooker and Buddy Guy are touring all round the world, putting records out on major labels, that's great. Everybody's working, and people know the music is here. It's a better situation than we've had for years.

RL Burnside:

We still get as many people round here listening to Blues as we ever did. In fact, when I started out, round here was mostly drum [1] music, there wasn't many people playing the guitar at all. Course later on when I went out to Chicago and Muddy Waters was playing, that was a big thing. But back here the youngsters like the Blues as much as they like rock and that other stuff. My kids, that's the music they like playing best.

Buddy Guy:

I have to tell people about this music, to carry things on. But they are some shoes to fill. Lightnin' Hopkins' shoes, Muddy Waters' shoes, BB's shoes, Howlin' Wolf's shoes, those shoes will stay there until eternal life, 'cause nobody is ever going to fill them. We may play, we may sound good, but there's no nobody gonna fill those shoes that those guys left. Before Mud passed, he told me to keep this music alive, and that is what I am trying to do. And when DJs aren't playing Blues music, when they are playing every crazy kind of music but the Blues, that isn't always easy, but I have to go out there and tell people who Muddy is, who T-Bone is, 'cause these people are important. I always think that the guy that made the shoe should be able to wear the shoe. BB, Muddy, Sonny Boy, they electrified the harmonica and the guitar, and those guys as far as I'm concerned are the fathers of what we're all doing now. Whenever you hear amplified guitar, or drums, or harmonica, that came from them. That's their title and they should hold it and they should be credited for it.

People are turning back to this music now – maybe it's because they're catching hell with the economy. There's a lot more people now beginning to realise what Blues is about. Blues songwriters listen to conversations around the world. I'll hear conversations from British people, Japanese people, and any nationality you go to, people got a problem. Sit in an airport, go to a restaurant or go to a bar and just listen. And as long as you can understand what they saying, you say, wow man, this has happened to me too. People say it's all sad, but it's not all sad. If you listen to BB King, I've got a sweet little angel, I love the way she spreads her wings – that's not sad. That is like saying this is a joyful thing, clap my hands and stamp my feet, 'cause this is a joyful time. But you have to just understand what we're saying. We singing exactly what's happening to you today, tonight and

149

R.L. Burnside

David Redfern / Redferns

Buddy Guy at Theresa's, Chicago 1971

yesterday. Sure we say about my baby left me this morning, and we also sing about the one that came home this morning. Matter of fact, when I first came to Chicago, people was doing all this work in the stockyards and the steel mills. People I hear complaining now, man I ain't been working in 13, 15 years – you didn't hear that then. They didn't have a worry in the world, their family was fed, rent was paid. But they still could understand the Blues. And now you got people sleeping in the street. It's still time for the Blues.

Homesick James:

It's much different these days, like I'm always saying to these youngsters, it's night and day, a different generation. They changed the thing all around. My mother had a strange way of playing in them old days, open strings, any way they wanted to tune it up. Now they just play 440 pitch. But they ain't playing the right Blues. Not like the Blues I experienced. Leadbelly, Patton, people like that, all the old guys, we changed it a little bit from them. But now it's gone completely out of control. Like the way they're playing guitar now, I wouldn't even pick a guitar up if I was starting now. All those computers and everything. A man don't need all that junk.

Larry Garner:

The future of the Blues is in the young folks – who are very critical. Back in the old days, like those old Louisiana guys, they played it all pretty much in the same way, they played

Elester Anderson and daughter, Tarboro North Carolina 1972

Jacob Stuckey and friends, Bentonia Mississippi 1973

Willie Johnson outside a juke joint near Elm City North Carolina 1972

it in Open E, and one song whether it was fast or slow it pretty much sounded like one long song! Unless you were into that type of music you would get bored real quick, you needed a variation and I think more and more guys are into writing their own songs and there are so many other influences from television and radio. The whole audience now is more critical, because there's more choice in terms of listening, and because CDs are expensive, and the performances are more expensive to get into. But I think more and more people, younger and older, who never listened to the Blues, are now at the point where they can open their mind to a real Blues tune, and can say this is what I have been missing all this time. But if you ain't delivering, young folks will let you know – and I think it is going to purify it, filter the crap out of the Blues as it rises.

Magic Slim:

People, you know, they don't always support the Blues like they should. The most people now who support the Blues is the white people. It's a few blacks, but you can see for yourself, it's mostly the white people. The Blues come from the black man but they don't support it. The white man, he support it, and that's the one making the money off the Blues. The black kids, they're into this here rock, and this stuff with talking going on, what you call it, rap, and rock and drugs, and that's why they can't support the Blues. They are the Blues, but they won't support it.

Yazoo City Mississippi 1974

Lonnie Brooks:

When I started with Alligator records most of the crowd would be, say, a hundred per cent white. Sometimes in some places there'd be about ten per cent black people in there, very few. Now more are coming out now than they used to. Specially when I play Chicago, you see about 25 per cent black in the place but it's still mostly white people listening to Blues now. And that doesn't bother me. I remember the time when we used to play these Blues clubs where it was all black and wait all night to get my money, I'd get through at four o'clock in the morning and I had to wait until six o'clock to get my money. Then we'd play white clubs and sometimes the guys would say, I'm not gonna be here tonight when you get off so here's your money now. Before that the club owners had you right under their thumb and they would do you and you wouldn't even know, but we got treated better when we played in some of the white clubs. I hate to say that but it's the truth.

Jr Kimbrough:

The youngsters in the city, they don't know nothing about the Blues too much – they were raised up on rock and rap and all that stuff. But these younger guys in the country, they are used to the Blues – some of the youngsters like Blues better than the ones that likes rock and rap. The older people like blues anyway, they come and hear it. We get youngsters and older people in my club. And there is a bunch of whites, they come down to hear the Blues too. And people out in Italy and Holland, I've been there too. It don't bother me.

When I started out the first songs I learnt was the old ones. 'Old Black Mattie', that is one of them, 'Shake 'em Down Baby', that is another one, and all that kind of music. That is what I come up on, and that was what I started playing. Then I got to starting playing other people's music, different kinds of music that I heard on the radio. And then I realised and understand that to get somewhere you got to do your own kind of music, there be no point fooling with this other stuff – there was no way I could make no music from anyone else's songs. I can play almost like any record that is out there, but it ain't doing me no good to play behind that. So I just started writing my own songs and putting my own music to it. I would just sit down, and they come in my mind. My songs, they have just the one chord, there's none of that fancy stuff you hear now, with lots of chords in one song. If I find another chord I leave it for another song. My songs don't come from the music I hear outside. It comes from inside myself. And that's why I seem to be doing pretty good with it these days. I'm not saying that is the way that everybody should be playing, but it's done pretty good for me.

Robert Stroger:

When you were a young kid you always wanted to be looked up to, that's why you got into music. And to get the girls. When I got into music it didn't change my girls – I still didn't get none – but I still got lots of respect from peoples. I never dreamed I would be a professional musician, that I'd be playing with musicians like Otis, and when you play with someone like him and he's on, boy he puts tears in your eyes, and it is a privilege to be there. But this is a business with me – that's the only way to keep going. It's a job I love to do, but I went into this just like a business, like you would open a restaurant. I had to put things aside to open up this business, and when I do fairly decent I put it back in the business, and then when things go slow I grab it out. Just like you would running a grocery store or a tavern.

John Lee Hooker:

In the Sixties the Blues was really big, and I think it's bigger now. It's really took over, everybody doing it. But I would say it's harder for musicians starting out now, 'cause there's so many of them now. Back then it wasn't that many. There's so many of them (now), whoo, and so many of them's good too, so the people in nightclubs they really can pick and choose. The nightclubs and record companies can really pick and choose, you say no, they say we can get somebody else just as good. It make it hard competition for every musician, they all trying to get on, but have a hard time doing it because the clubs and records are picky. There's so many of them out there – if you don't do it, somebody else will. Back then it was scarce.

I don't know what has made me last longer than other people. It comes with a feeling, a talent, experience – you've got to feel it. I can't explain it myself. It's just there. There was times when it was hard, but I keep on at it. Like I told you, you got to keep pushing.

It is easier for me now than it used to be. I will do one show now – back then I would do four or five. I like hanging out at my house, driving cars, watching baseball. I got a lot of cars. Sometimes I play guitar around the house. Not too much. Making records is no

153

Willie Guy Rainey and friend, Palmetto Georgia 1978

problem. I do it and I get out of there. One take and go. Oh yeah. Just one take. Now I can't comment on how other musicians make records. No comment. Each to his own. That's the way they want it, and that's the way I want it. It depends. That's what they do. I got mine, and that's what I do. That's the way I always done it, and that is how I'm gonna keep on doing it.

Jimmy Rogers:

Rock and roll, soul, hip hop and all that stuff, that's a quick here right now thing, and that jumps in the front of the Blues, 'cause everybody's grabbing at that fast buck. But it's come easy go easy, that's the way it is. Very few stands out and make a career of it — you hear a guy this month, then you don't hear from him no more. I noticed down through the years that that's the way the cookie crumbles. I got me a base to work from — I'm not gonna leave and go someplace else. Man, I enjoy playing, I enjoy travelling. I gets bored even in Chicago where I was raised up, my roots is in that area — but I gets bored. Two weeks, nothing to do 'cept twiddle your thumbs and go fishing, that gets boring, the fish don't be biting, oh man I wanna hit the road and get out here. I don't like to stay in one place, I likes to keep moving. I love that road.

Chapter 11 – Notes

1:      'drum': ie the fife and drum music practised by Sid Hemphill and others

John Lee Hooker rehearsing for 'Ready Steady Go!' TV show, London 1964

Billy Boy Arnold

(Born 16 September 1935, Chicago)
Billy Boy played harmonica on the Chicago streets with Ellas McDaniel, nick-naming the latter Bo Diddley after an eccentric performer at the Indiana Theatre. When Bo Diddley signed to Chess in 1955, Leonard Chess was not interested in his sideman, so Billy Boy signed to Chicago label Vee Jay and recorded many Blues/R&B classics including 'I Wish You Would' and 'I Ain't Got You', which would become staples of the British R&B movement. Although he largely retired from the music industry in the Sixties and Seventies – he says he was disillusioned with his own playing – Billy Boy made a welcome return with his album 'Back Where I Belong' (ALCD4815) for Alligator.

Roosevelt 'Booba' Barnes

(Born 26 September 1936, Longwood, Miss)
Barnes is best known via his juke joint, the Playboy Club, in Greenville Mississippi, where he regularly performed throughout the Eighties, with an exuberant stage act he says outdoes his hero Howlin' Wolf. Over the last couple of years Barnes has spent much of his time performing in Chicago. Recommended: 'Heartbroken Man' (Rooster Blues 72623)

Lonnie Brooks

(Born 18 December 1933, Dubuisson La)
Born Lee Baker, as a youth Brooks improvised a charcoal moustache to help him look old enough to get into Gatemouth Brown club dates. His first major musical engagement was playing guitar with Zydeco legend Clifton Chenier. He enjoyed local success as Guitar Jr with the singles 'Family Rules' and 'The Crawl', before moving to Chicago in 1960 and taking up the Brooks moniker – there was already one Guitar Jr playing the local clubs. From there it was a hard ride until he hooked up with Alligator Records in 1978, since when his fame has steadily increased, aided by his 'dang, that ain't the Blues' appearance on Heineken beer commercials. Brooks now enjoys a reputation as one of the best live performers on the Blues circuit. Recommended: 'Bayou Lightning' (Alligator AL4714)

Clarence Gatemouth Brown

(Born April 18 1924, Vinton La)
Brown's influence in Louisiana and Texas Blues is ubiquitous: he inspired countless guitarists including Albert Collins, Guitar Slim and Jimmie Vaughan. Brown's career took off when he spontaneously picked up T-Bone Walker's guitar and started playing while the latter took a break during a gig at the Bronze Peacock in Texas. The Peacock's manager, Don Robey, took the young Gate under his wing, securing him a contract with Aladdin, and then setting up his own record company, Peacock. According to Brown: 'Robey told me, I'm going to make you famous, and me rich. And that's exactly what happened.' After a number of regional hits, Brown went on to varied musical activities including acting as bandleader on black music show The Beat, and a stint playing Country music in Nashville. A recent record deal with the Verve label and tours with Eric Clapton have, belatedly, brought the still feisty Mr Brown back to the public eye – now in his seventies, Gate is not retiring in any sense of the world. Recommended: 'His Peacock Recordings' (Rounder 2039); The Man (Verve 523 761-2)

Eddie Burns

(Born 8 1928, February Belzoni Miss)
Eddie 'Guitar' Burns started out playing harmonica with Sonny Boy Williamson II before moving to Detroit in 1948 and teaming up with John Lee Hooker. Burns played guitar on many of Hooker's early recordings, as well as later Chess tracks such as 'One Scotch, One Bourbon And One Beer'. During the late Sixties Burns was tied up in an abortive deal with Motown, contracted to the label for nine years without any releases, but his R&B following in the city endured to the extent that he even helped Mr Hooker get gigs in Detroit in the Seventies. Recommended: 'Detroit' (Evidence ECD 26024). Burns also has one solo track and one track with Hooker on the box set 'Chess Blues' (MCA/Chess CHD4-9340)

RL Burnside

(Born 23 November 1926, Oxford Miss)
RL has been playing Mississippi Blues for the last 50 years, but has only lately come to widespread attention via his deal with Mississippi label Fat Possum and his appearance on the Deep Blues film and video. Burnside plays with the spirit of an early Muddy Waters, and like his Fat Possum label mate Jr Kimbrough there's an eerie edge about his playing that sets him apart – and corrects the impression that Blues is a dying art-form. Recommended: 'Bad Luck City' (Fat Possum/ Demon 741)

Robert 'Catman' Catfrey

Catman has been playing tenor saxophone for various New Orleans outfits since the Forties, as well as leading his own band, Catman And His Kittens. His first major job was playing saxophone for Guitar Slim, with whom he also toured. Catman's sidelines included MC'ing at the city's legendary Dew Drop Inn, and acting as the club's official photographer.

Boozoo Chavis

(Born 23 October 1930, Lake Charles La)
Wilson 'Boozoo' Chavis grew up playing French and Blues music on the harmonica and accordion, and was playing regularly at Lake Charles clubs by the mid Forties. In 1954 Chavis made one of the first recordings in the Blues/Cajun hybrid which would become famous as Zydeco, or Zodeco (a name thought to have been derived from the Cajun phrase 'les haricots sont pas salés', or 'the beans aren't salted'). 'Paper In My Shoe' was a regional hit, predating Clifton Chenier's first success, but Chenier's exuberant stage act would overshadow Chenier throughout most of his career, which was in the doldrums throughout the Seventies. Boozoo now records regularly for the Rounder label, and still packs them in in the Louisiana clubs. Recommended: 'Boozoo's Breakdown' (Sonet 1042)

Albert Collins

(Born 1 October 1932 Leona Tx)
Flash in both dress sense and playing style, Albert Collins made his name the hard way, playing constantly around Texas and the South, and scoring a regional hit with 'The Freeze', before teaming up with Blues-Rock group Canned Heat, who helped sign him to the Imperial label in 1968. Unfortunately, by 1972, internecine disputes within Imperial caused him to be ousted from the label, and his career took a downturn which forced him to scrape a living driving trucks and even decorating Neil Diamond's house. Salvation appeared in 1977, in the shape of the Alligator label, for whom he recorded a string of successful albums, while a Live Aid performance in 1985 underlined his international appeal. Sadly for a man to whom success and respect came late in life, Collins succumbed to lung cancer in 1993. Recommended: 'Ice Pickin'' (Alligator CD4713); 'Showdown' (Alligator CD4743); 'Collins Mix' (Virgin PointBlank CD17)

James Cotton

(Born 1 July 1935, Tunica Miss)
James Cotton has been active in many of the key phases of modern Blues, playing with Sonny Boy Williamson on the influential King Biscuit Time show in Helena Arkansas, taking up harmonica duties with Muddy Waters in what many regard as one of his best live bands, and being at the forefront of the move to the West Coast as white audiences embraced the Blues. While Cotton's fame has not reached the heights of some contemporaries, he at least has never been out of the frame, recording for Sun in the Fifties, Chess, Verve and Vanguard in the Sixties, Buddah in the Seventies, Alligator and Antone's in the Eighties, and Verve in the Nineties! Recommended: 'Live At Antone's' (Antone's ANTCD0007)

Robert Cray

(Born 1 August 1953, Columbus Ga)
A man who demonstrated that Blues could still sound contemporary in the age of the drum machine, Cray, like many American teenagers, was inspired to play the guitar by the example of the Beatles. Later on Cray started investigating his parents' Blues record collection, while a meeting with Albert Collins at a high school hop proved fateful. Cray formed a Blues band, one incarnation of which would end up backing Collins. Following constant touring, and an abortive album recorded for Tomato, but not released for two years, Cray started to win widespread attention, not least from Eric Clapton, who covered the title track of Cray's Hightone release, 'Bad Influence'. Within three years Cray had signed to Mercury and crossed over to mainstream appeal with 'Strong Persuader', accused by critics of purveying yuppie Blues, but embraced by a world-wide audience. Recommended: (with Albert Collins) 'Showdown' (Alligator CD4743); 'Strong Persuader' (Mercury 830 568-2)

CeDell Davis

(Born 9 June 1927, Helena Arkansas)
Growing up in Helena, it wasn't a surprise that guitarist CeDell should fall in with Sonny Boy Williamson II, Robert Nighthawk or Houston Stackhouse, all of them regulars on the KFFA scene. Davis had to overcome more hurdles than most of his contemporaries, however, for a childhood attack of polio forced him to completely alter his playing technique, turning the guitar around to play it left handed, and using a knife as a slider. The result is haunting but outlandish – and, to some conventionalists, out of tune. Davis moved to Pine Bluff with Robert Nighthawk in the Sixties, where he remained until a move to Nashville in 1995; a recent deal with the Fat Possum label has brought him more attention – and none too late. Recommended: Feel Like Doin' Something Wrong (Fat Possum/ Demon FIEND-CD745)

Willie Dixon

(Born 1 July 1915, Vicksburg Miss)
A songwriter supreme and omnipresent figure in the development of Chicago Blues, Willie Dixon was part of the pre-electric Chicago scene with The Big Three, was involved as bassist, writer and virtual producer on many of the most popular Chess records played by Muddy Waters, Howlin Wolf, Little Walter, Chuck Berry and others, and by assisting Otis Rush and Buddy Guy early in their careers played a large part in the rise of what would be termed the 'West Side Sound'. To some extent Dixon was a hustler, aiming to get his songs covered by a wide variety of musicians. But the artists who recorded his songs did themselves as much of a favour as they did Dixon, for he was a musical visionary who had a great ear for a single, and helped make much of the output of Chess and Cobra Records some of the finest popular music of all time. Willie died in 1992. Recommended: 'Hidden Charms' (Silvertone CD515); 'A Tribute To Willie Dixon' (Charly CD RED7); 'The Chess Box' (MCA CHD2-1650)

David 'Honeyboy' Edwards

(Born 28 June 1915, Shaw Miss)
Honeyboy Edwards has experienced most phases of the Blues first-hand, hoboing as a Delta Bluesman around the South, playing in Memphis during the heyday

of the jug bands, and finally moving to Chicago and recording for Chess during its electric era. But Edwards shouldn't be dismissed as a fellow traveller – even at the age of 80, his best live performances are simply electrifying. Oblivious to the crowd, Edwards simply plays for his own pleasure, leaving spaces that are as eloquent as the notes, and occasionally can be seen smiling gnomically to himself as he puts a new spin on a 70-year old song. Recommended: 'Delta Bluesman' (Earwig 4922)

Lowell Fulson
(Born 31 March 1921, Tulsa OK)
In his youth Lowell Fulson listened to Blues, Country, and the eclectic violin playing of his African-born grandfather (and adopted Choctaw medicine man) Henry Fulson. Fulson played with veteran Bluesman Texas Alexander before being drafted for WWII, but after a close scrape with a submarine posting (which he escaped by demonstrating to his commanding officer that they could never replace his cooking skills) he and his Jump Blues combo entertained US troops on Guam. After his discharge Fulson became a full-time musician and recorded standards such as 'Three O'Clock In The Morning' and the definitive version of 'Everyday I Have The Blues', both of which would be recorded by BB King. Other hits followed, including 'Reconsider Baby', for Chess, and 'Tramp', for Kent', best known via the Otis Redding and Carla Thomas version. Fulson, who has recently been covered by Eric Clapton (on 'Cradle To The Grave') and Salt 'N' Pepa ('Tramp') and sampled by Prince ('7') now lives the quiet life in California, releasing occasional CDs for Bullseye. Recommended: 'Reconsider Baby' (Charly CDBM48); 'Hold On' (Bullseye 9525)

Larry Garner
(Born 8 July 1952, New Orleans La)
Garner grew up listening to and playing with Baton Rouge Bluesmen such as Lonesome Sundown and Tabby Thomas. His own brand of Blues, however, is far less down-home: thoughtful, and dedicated to modern concerns such as city life or the fatal charms of video poker machines. Garner's first album for the UK independent label JSP won him many plaudits as one of the finest songwriters working in the Blues genre, while in 1994 he finally achieved major label status via a contract with Verve. Recommended: 'You Need To Live A Little' (Verve 523 759-2)

Henry Gray
(Born 19 January 1925, Kenner Louisiana)
Best-known as the pianist for Howlin' Wolf from 1956 to 1968, Henry Gray also played live or recorded with Little Walter, Jimmy Rogers, Junior Wells, Jimmy Reed and Billy Boy Arnold, to name a few. Gray returned to his native Louisiana in 1969, and was one of the last artists to record for the Excello label. Gray still performs regularly in Europe and the US, as well as Baton Rouge's local Blues club, the Blues Box.

Buddy Guy
(Born 30 July 1936, Lettsworth La)
Guy's fame as an electrifying guitarist and singer is widespread, but his reputation was won the hard way via viciously competitive guitar cutting contests against the likes of Otis Rush and Magic Sam.
Guy played with fellow Louisiana performers such as Lazy Lester and Slim Harpo in his teens, but moved to Chicago after being supplied with a list of contacts by Baton Rouge DJ Diggy Doo. They all proved fruitless, but Guy's electrifying early performances, in which he borrowed many of Guitar Slim's on-stage antics, at the 708 Club, Theresa's Lounge and the Squeeze club soon brought him to the attention of Willie Dixon, Muddy Waters, and others. Dixon helped Guy sign to Artistic/Cobra records; after Cobra went bust Guy

moved to Chess, recording both as a session guitarist and under his own name, for hits such as 1962's 'Stone Crazy'. Guy's influence on Eric Clapton, in particular, was a factor in his appeal to white audiences, and while record company interest proved elusive in the Seventies and Eighties Guy could still draw a crowd, particularly when teamed up with long-time partner Jr Wells. Recently Guy has managed to convert his hard-won credibility into record sales following a deal with the Silvertone label, and albums such as 'Damn Right I Got The Blues', 'Feels Like Rain' and 'Slippin' In'. Recommended: 'Stone Crazy' (Roots CD33010); 'Slippin' In' (Silvertone 533)

Jessie Mae Hemphill
(Born 6 October 1934, Senatobia Miss)
Jessie Mae Hemphill is the inheritor of a musical tradition handed down from grandfather Sid Hemphill, which some commentators believe derives directly from Africa. According to Jessie, Sid's father, Doc Hemphill, originated from New Orleans, one of the few places in the USA where drums, thought to incite rebellion, were tolerated. Sid Hemphill played violin, fife, drums and many other instruments, and the young Jessie Mae accompanied him, usually on snare or bass drum, on many local picnic and parties. Hemphill has continued in Sid's footsteps by playing the distinctive Marshall country fife and drum music, with local fife player Napoleon Strickland, while also playing her own brand of guitar-based Blues. Recommended: Hemphill is featured on the excellent compilation 'Deep Blues' (Anxious 4509-91981-2)

Homesick James
(Born 3 May 1910, Somerville Tenn)
The cousin of celebrated electric slide player Elmore James, Homesick started out playing Delta blues, but made the transition to urban music well before many of his contemporaries. John Williamson, as he was born, hobo'd through Carolina and Mississippi with Blind Boy Fuller and others before settling in Chicago in 1930. Over subsequent years James would work with Big Joe Williams, Sonny Boy Williamson I, Albert King and many others, but his most lasting collaboration would be with Elmore James. Homesick played bass or six string guitar on some of James' mid-Fifties sessions for Flair, and most of his later recordings for the Fire and Enjoy labels, before Elmore died of a heart attack in Homesick's Chicago apartment in 1963. Since then Homesick has toured both as a solo 'Delta'-style singer, and with an electric band. Recommended: 'Goin' Back In The Times' (Earwig 4929); 'Blues On The Southside' (Original Blues Recordings CD529)

John Lee Hooker
(Born 22 August 1920, Clarksdale Miss)
One of the giants of post-War Blues, Hooker has retained his pre-eminent position by sheer tenacity. When he shot to fame with 'Boogie Chillen' in 1948, Hooker's reputation as a bright young thing was ironically rooted in the fact that he represented a return to tradition. Hooker, Muddy Waters and Lightnin' Hopkins represented a revolutionary electric triumvirate, who would supersede the likes of Big Bill Broonzy or Memphis Minnie, yet an intrinsic part of their appeal was that they reminded urban workers of the down-home Delta Blues they'd heard in their youth. However, while Hooker's fame was based on tradition, the man was always ready to move with the times, as was shown when he teamed up with boogie guitarist Eddie Taylor for his Vee Jay recordings in 1955; resulting songs such as 'Boom Boom' and 'Dimples' gave him a new wave of hits, and a new wave of English fans. Over subsequent years Hooker rode the wave of the folk Blues revival, and teamed up with Canned Heat to make the crossover to Rock audiences in 1970. By the late Eighties, however, Hooker's career looked to be in

irretrievable decline when manager Mike Kappus paid for the recording of an album of duets with the likes of Bonnie Raitt and Robert Cray. After being turned down by every major US label, Kappus pulled off a deal with US independent label Chameleon, and Silvertone in the UK. The resulting album, 'The Healer', was a surprise hit, eventually selling over one million copies – despite the fact that Chameleon had initially been unwilling to press more than 50,000 copies of what they thought would be a marginal album. Since then the albums 'Mr Lucky', 'Boom Boom' and 'Chill Out' have scored similar mainstream success. Recommended: 'The Legendary Modern Recordings' (Ace CDCHD315); 'Chill Out' (Virgin PointBlank PBCD 22)

Bruce Iglauer
(Born 10 July 1947, Ann Arbor Michigan)
Founder of Chicago's Alligator Blues label, Bruce Iglauer has been an integral figure in the revival of Blues in the Eighties and Nineties. The inspiration for launching Alligator came when Iglauer saw rough and ready Chicago Bluesman Hound Dog Taylor play a Chicago bar; Taylor became the first act signed to the new label, initially run from Iglauer's Chicago apartment. Iglauer is a hands-on producer who closely supervises many Alligator sessions; the result of his attention to detail was a series of albums which in many cases captured artists at a new peak and brought the likes of Albert Collins, Lonnie Brooks and Koko Taylor back from the wilderness, while providing a vital first step for younger acts including Tinsley Ellis and Kenny Neal.

Willie Kent
(Born 24 September 1936, Shelby Miss)
Now that Magic Slim has moved out of the city, Willie Kent has taken on the mantle of the hardest-working bandleader in Chicago, and can be seen at local clubs most nights of the week. Kent started out playing with a number of small groups, graduating to occasional live dates with Little Walter, Muddy Waters and Howlin' Wolf, but his role as a bassist has impeded his success as a frontman. However, following recent albums recorded for Wolf and Delmark, a measure of international attention and success is belatedly coming his way. Recommended: 'Ain't It Nice'(Delmark DD653)

BB King
(Born 16 September 1925, Indianola Miss)
If BB King looks conspicuously successful, it is a status that has been earned the hard way. When radio play proved elusive as Rock 'n' Roll hit in the mid Fifties, BB King bought a bus and started touring. He's been on the road ever since, and has become the Blues' greatest ambassador, as well as one of the most influential guitarists of all time.
Riley King started out as a conventional Delta guitarist, but despite loving the slide sound of players such as his relative Bukka White, could never quite handle a bottleneck. Aiming to capture the vocal quality of the slide guitar, King developed a uniquely expressive and versatile style, which took in the more sophisticated influences of Louis Jordan or T-Bone Walker, and which would heavily influence Rock and Blues musicians alike. After some abortive early recordings for the Bullet label, King hit his stride with a string of releases for the Modern label in the Fifties. As the white Blues boom hit King was somewhat overlooked, but the inspired decision by new record company ABC to capture a typical King performance on a live album recorded at the Chicago Regal Theatre in 1964 resulted in one of the finest albums of the decade. The innovatory step of putting strings on a Blues records, for 1968's 'The Thrill Is Gone', produced King's first crossover hit, since when he has continued to play for sell-out crowds for 300 nights a year. Recommended: 'King Of The Blues' (MCAD4-10677); 'Best Of' (Ace CDCH908); 'Live At The Regal' (BGO CD235/Ace CH86)

Earl King

(Born 7 February 1934, New Orleans La)
Earl King has been described as 'one of New Orleans' finest songwriters, one of the city's best guitarists, and the proud owner of the wildest hair in Louisiana.' Guilty on all three counts. King started out as a disciple of the notorious Guitar Slim before scoring hits of his own such as 'Those Lonely Lonely Nights', 'Trick Bag' and 'Come On Let The Good Times Roll'. From the Sixties King spent much of his time writing for and producing other artists – his songs have been covered by figures as diverse as Jimi Hendrix and Professor Longhair. King's latest albums for the New Orleans label Blacktop show that he is one of the finest songwriters working in any genre, let alone the Blues. Recommended: 'Sexual Telepathy' (Blacktop/ Demon FIENDCD168); 'Hard River To Cross' (Blacktop 1090)

Jr Kimbrough

(Born 28 July 1930, Hudsonville Miss)
Senior figures in the Blues industry have described David Jr Kimbrough's music as out-of-tune, primitive and disturbing – which means it must be worth investigating. Kimbrough runs what is probably Mississippi's most legendary juke joint near Holly Springs Mississippi, at which he and RL Burnside are the most regular attractions. His debut album 'All Night Long', produced by Rolling Stone writer Robert Palmer, and recorded in Jr's club, is quite possibly the finest Blues recording of the decade – his music revolves around brooding repetitive riffs, and while he's as authentically down-home as John Lee Hooker, Kimbrough's sound seems to combine trace elements of Indian ragas, psychedelia or even the grungy guitar boogie of ZZ Top. Recommended:'All Night Long' (Fat Possum/ Demon FIENDCD742)

Eddie Kirkland

(Born 16 August 1928, Jamaica, West Indies)
Accompanying John Lee Hooker is one of the most difficult tasks to face any musician, but it is one which Kirkland carried off with ease. Kirkland grew up in Alabama, and recalls sitting at the feet of Blind Blake as he played guitar, before leaving home to join the Sugar Girls Medicine Show in 1940. After the show split up, Kirkland moved around Detroit and Indiana, at one point making a living as a boxer, before settling in Detroit and meeting Hooker at a house party in 1947. Kirkland was Hooker's most frequent accompanist until the Boogie man started working with Eddie Taylor during his stint on Vee Jay, at which point Kirkland moved to backing Soul artists such as Otis Redding. Kirkland and Hooker teamed up again in 1967 for the Bluesway label, since when Kirkland has pursued a solo career. Recommended:' All Around The World' (Deluge3001)

Sam Lay

(Born 20 March 1935, Birmingham Al)
Sam Lay came to Chicago in 1960, but despite his late arrival on the scene soon won a reputation of being, along with Fred Below, the most in-demand drummer in the city. Lay's unbeatable CV includes work with most of the Chicago greats including Muddy Waters, Howlin' Wolf, Little Walter, and John Lee Hooker, while via his work with the Butterfield Blues Band and Bob Dylan he was at the centre of the move which saw Blues taken up by white audiences. Lay still plays regularly in the US and Europe with his own band. Recommended:'The Paul Butterfield Blues Band' (Elektra 960 647-2)

SP Leary

(Born 6 June 1930, Dallas Tx)
SP Leary played drums with electric guitar pioneer T-Bone Walker in the Texas clubs while still in his teens. SP moved to Chicago in 1954 and was soon playing West Side clubs with Sonny Boy Williamson II and Johnny Shines. SP recorded with Jimmy Rogers, Magic Sam, Elmore James, Muddy Waters, Howlin' Wolf and John Lee Hooker, and continued playing regular club dates until the early Nineties. Since then ill-health has sadly forced him to substantially curtail his playing.

Little Milton

(Born 7 September 1934, Inverness Miss)
Little Milton Campbell is not one of the best-known names to white Blues fans, but his recordings for the Malaco label demonstrate his brand of soul-drenched Blues still have a healthy following in the American South. Milton's original ambition was to emulate T-Bone Walker, and in fact much of his early work for the Trumpet and Sun labels shows him still struggling to find an original voice. By the Sixties, and his hit records with Bobbin and Chess, Milton started to find his own style, and his own audience. Since then Milton has continued to do his own thing, and while white audiences embrace the likes of Otis Rush, on whom he was a significant influence, he still makes a good living playing the chitlin circuit. Recommended: 'Tending His Roots' (Charly CDRB17)

Robert Lockwood Jr

(Born 27 March 1915, Marvell Ar)
Robert Lockwood is usually judged famous by association – he was the adopted son of Robert Johnson, from whom he learned guitar, and the accompanist to many greats including Sonny Boy Williamson II and Little Walter. In fact Lockwood was immensely influential – he was probably the main figure to popularise the electric guitar in Mississippi, and BB King learned guitar techniques from him in the Forties. Lockwood was later one of the most ubiquitous session guitarists for Chess, although sadly for us his distrust of the label meant he made relatively few recordings under his own name. Recommended: (with Johnny Shines) 'Hangin' On' (Rounder 2023); 'Chess Blues' (MCA/Chess CHD4-9340)

Magic Slim

(Born 7 August 1937, Grenada Miss)
One of the hardest-working artists in Chicago, Magic Slim has been playing his no-frills Blues in the city's clubs for over 30 years. Born Morris Holt, Slim went to school with future West Side pioneer Magic Sam; the hefty Mr Holt moved to Chicago around 1955, shortly after Sam, and was given his new name while playing bass in Sam's band. However, the young Slim found the Chicago club scene too intimidating, and moved back to Grenada for five years before returning to the city and forming his own band, the Tear Drops, with brother Nick Holt on bass. Like most of the city's other Bluesmen, Slim made the move to playing mostly Northside clubs from the Seventies. He's been playing his authentic, solid Blues, which on exceptionally loud nights bring to mind Canned Heat or ZZ Top, ever since. Recommended: 'Grand Slam' (Rooster Blues 2618)

John Mayall

(Born 29 November 1933, Manchester UK)
One of the prime architects in the rise of British Blues, John Mayall was also integral to the development of Sixties Rock music, via his fostering of guitar talents such as Eric Clapton, Peter Green, and Mick Taylor. By all accounts a strict boss, Mayall was a gifted writer and arranger who wisely allowed his guitar charges a full share of the limelight, and was rewarded with critical and commercial successes such as 'Blues Breakers' (London 800 086-2) with Clapton, and 'A Hard Road' (London 820 474-2) with Green, who would go on to record some of the finest British Blues with Fleetwood Mac. Mayall's recent 'Silvertone' albums demonstrate he still retains his skills as a bandleader and talent spotter.

Cosimo Matassa

(Born 13 April 1926, New Orleans La)
Matassa was the recording king of New Orleans, responsible for putting on tape (or acetate) some of the very best records by Big Joe Turner, Little Richard, Guitar Slim, Elmore James and many more influential performers from the late Forties onwards. The modest Matassa, who now runs a grocery store in the French Quarter, claims he never had a trademark sound, but would merely go into the recording room, listen to how the band sounded, and then capture that sound on tape. If only some modern producers would follow his example...

Jay Miller

(Born 5 May 1922, Iopa Louisiana)
JD Miller was one of the most influential figures in the development of Louisiana Blues in the Fifties. Miller started out as a Cajun and Western Swing musician, then turned his hand to production. After he discovered Lightning Slim and started licensing his records to the Nashville Excello label, Miller became known for the 'Excello Sound' – languid, low-down infectious Blues in a Jimmy Reed stylee, which would have a profound influence on British R&B groups such as the Stones and the Yardbirds. Excello's financial affairs were complicated in the extreme, with Miller claiming to have received minimal payments from Nashville, and the musicians claiming to have received minimal payments from Miller. Still, the records were great. Recommended: 'Excello Authentic R&B' (Ace CDCH D492)

Dave Myers

(Born 30 October 1926, Byhalia Miss)
Dave Myers and his brother Louis formed the Aces with Jr Wells and drummer Fred Below around 1948, soon gaining a reputation as one of the most swinging bands in Chicago. However, it was Little Walter who brought the band to real prominence, hiring the Aces as his backing band when he left Muddy Waters – in a neat exchange, Wells became Walter's replacement in the Waters band. Dave, as one of the first electric bassists in the city, and Louis subsequently backed up the likes of Otis Rush and even Louis Jordan. David Myers continues to work occasionally with the likes of Billy Boy Arnold and Jimmy Rogers. Recommended: (with Little Walter) 'Blues With A Feeling' (Charly CD BM23)

Jack Owens

(Born 17 November 1904, Bentonia Miss)
Owens is one of the last surviving exponents of the Bentonia Blues style exemplified by Skip James, using a minor-tuned guitar to accompany haunting high-pitched vocal lines. Where James was a professional musician who hoboed around the South, Owens was less adventurous, and rarely left the village where he was born. Although many of his songs are derived directly from James' originals, his occasional live performances, and recordings for the Wolf label, demonstrate he is an arresting performer in his own right. Recommended: (with Eugene Powell) 'Last Giants Of Mississippi Blues' (Wolf 120.931)

Sonny Payne

(Born 29 November 1924, Helena Arkansas)
Sonny Payne joined the then-fledgling KFFA radio station in Helena Arkansas in 1941, and by 1942 was working as an announcer on the hugely-influential *King Biscuit Time* show with Sonny Boy Williamson II and Robert Lockwood Jr. A break followed when Payne entered the services, and subsequently joined a Western Swing Band, but in 1950 Payne rejoined KFFA and took over the *King Biscuit Time* show. Payne presents *King Biscuit Time* to this day; it is now broadcast from Helena's Delta Cultural Centre.

Eugene Powell

(Born 23 December 1908, Utica Miss)
Little-known outside his native Greenville, Powell worked in Memphis in the late Twenties and started to make a name for himself at the Savoy Club in Beale St, playing duets with a guitarist named Richard 'Hacksaw' Harney - according to Powell, an integral part of their act would be a duet with Harney playing in G and Powell in A flat, a piece of musical footwork that must have been nimble in the extreme. Powell recorded as Sonny Boy Nelson with his wife Mississippi Matilda in 1936 at the behest of Bo Carter, but then slipped into obscurity. He would not record again until 1971. His 1993 recordings for the Wolf label demonstrate that he is still a formidable guitarist. Recommended: (with Jack Owens) 'Last Giants Of Mississippi Blues' (Wolf 120.931)

Yank Rachell

(Born 16 March 1910, Brownsville Tenn)
Most Blues instrumentalists have made their fame with the guitar, piano or harmonica, but Yank Rachell rules the rarefied roost of Blues mandolin players, and has particularly influenced Ry Cooder. Rachell met up with Sleepy John Estes in Brownsville in 1919, and the two soon hit the road together, travelling through the Mississippi Delta. Estes and Rachell were in Memphis in the late Twenties at the time of the jug band craze, and recorded for the Victor label. The two separated around 1930, when Rachell returned to farming before recording with Sonny Boy Williamson I in 1938. It would be the early Sixties, and the coffee bar Blues boom, before Rachell returned to music full time, when he teamed up once more with Sleepy John in a revived partnership that would last, on and off, until Estes' death in 1977. Yank has since been largely retired. Recommended: (with Sleepy John Estes) 'Brownsville Blues' (Delmark 613)

Keith Richards

(Born 18 December 1943, Dartford, Kent UK)
The 1964 debut album by Keith Richards' group, The Rolling Stones, was a definitive primer for American blues – all 12 of its songs were covers of artists such as Jimmy Reed, Chuck Berry, or Slim Harpo. To a white audience, of course, this was something new, radical, and dangerous. While his group have since attained the status of a major multinational company, Richards has stayed true to his roots by playing with Blues musicians including John Lee Hooker, Chuck Berry and Johnnie Johnson. Recommended: 'The Rolling Stones' (London 8200842); 'Let It Bleed' (London 8200852)

Tommy Ridgley

(Born 30 October 1925 New Orleans La)
One of New Orleans' best-kept secrets, singer and pianist Tommy Ridgley came to fame when he was hired by Dave Bartholomew in 1949. Ridgley recorded for Imperial the same year and scored his first hit with Shrewesbury Blues. Over subsequent years Ridgley and his band The Untouchables would record for several labels, including Atlantic, but never managed to break out of New Orleans. Still a popular attraction at the city's local clubs and annual Heritage Festival, Ridgley has recently signed to the city's Black Top label. Recommended: 'How Long' (Sound Of New Orleans 1024)

Jimmy Rogers

(Born 3 June 1924, Atlanta Ga)
Jimmy Rogers was inspired to pick up the guitar by Blind Lemon Jefferson and Big Bill Broonzy, and by 1940 had made his way to Helena, Arkansas and was hanging out with the likes of Sunnyland Slim, and King Biscuit Time guitarist Joe Willie Wilkin. By the time Rogers made his way to Chicago in 1941, Wilkin and Robert Lockwood Jr had inspired him to take up the newly-invented electric guitar – thus when Rogers teamed up for live dates with the newly-arrived Muddy Waters in 1945, it was natural they should have an all-electric band.

Rogers would not actually record with Waters until 1950, by which time the band's personnel, including Little Walter on harp, were notorious for blowing lesser competition off stage. The first Waters lineup was, of course, responsible for a string of memorable singles such as 'Hoochie Coochie Man' and 'Got My Mojo Working'. Rogers released several popular singles under his own name during his time with Waters, including 1950's Luedella. By 1955, and his best-known single Walking By Myself, Rogers had left the Waters band; he subsequently worked occasionally with Howlin' Wolf and Sonny Boy Williamson, but lacking a natural band leader's temperament never managed to sustain his own group, and by 1960 had largely retired from the music business. From 1970 onwards Rogers returned to performing, and he is now more active than ever, spending several months each year on tour. Recommended: 'That's All Right' (Charly CDRED15); 'Muddy Waters' Chess Box' (MCA/Chess CHD3-80003); 'Blue Bird' (Analogue Productions APO2001)

Otis Rush

(Born 29 April 1934, Philadelphia Miss)
Otis Rush's first recordings, made for the Cobra label between 1956 and 1958, are some of the finest Blues ever made – startlingly original, and still emotionally arresting 40 years after they were made. Tragically, from these superlative beginnings Rush's career has gone steadily downhill, his lack of self-confidence inhibiting his work to the point that his initial genius is only occasionally discernible behind workmanlike Albert King imitations. It was Rush's fruitless deals with both Chess and Duke records in the Sixties that caused him to lose the momentum of his Cobra years.
A collaboration with white Bluesmen Mike Bloomfield and Nick Gravenites could have brought him a white audience, but Rush was unhappy, referring to the recording venue, Muscle Shoals, Alabama as "Mus' I show up in Alabama?" Although compromised, the resulting 'Mourning In The Morning' (Atlantic 82367-2) still captures the Rush magic, and reminds how Cream and Fleetwood Mac in particular took him as a blueprint. Rush has toured internationally lately thanks to a record deal with This Way Up records, and both his recordings and his live dates must be worth investigating because when Rush plays Rush, he is truly without peer. Recommended: 'His Cobra Recordings' (Flyright FLYCD01)

Johnny Shines

(Born 15 April 1915, Frayser Tenn)
Best-known for his time on the road with Robert Johnson, Johnny Shines later became a major figure in the Chicago clubs. Shines met Johnson around 1935, and stayed on the road with him, off and on, for two years, during which they ventured as far afield as St Louis and even Canada, and appeared on The Elder Moten Hour radio show in Detroit, Michigan. Shines subsequently settled in Memphis, while Johnson continued rambling, meeting his death in 1938. In 1941, Shines followed the example of many musicians from the South, moving to Chicago and playing for tips on Maxwell Street. He would stay in the city for the next 25 years, becoming a regular in the city's clubs. Shines recorded for Chess and JOB, but the lack of financial success contributed to his retirement from music from 1957-1964. Shines subsequently made up for lost time by becoming a fixture on the club and Blues festival scene, playing his own authentic brand of Delta Blues, and acceding to the many demands for interpretations of songs by his Thirties travelling companion. Shines died in 1992. Recommended (with Robert Lockwood) 'Hangin' On' (Rounder 2023)

Roebuck 'Pops' Staples

(Born 28 December 1915, Winona Miss)
Pops Staples grew up on the Dockery plantation near Drew, Mississippi; the plantation was home to Henry Sloan and Charley Patton, and in some quarters is regarded as the very birthplace of the Blues. Staples always played Gospel as well as the Blues, not that the dividing line in those early days was particularly distinct, but after moving with his wife and family to Chicago in 1934, stopped playing music for over a decade. By 1950 his children were old enough to sing with him in what would become the Staple Singers, one of the most influential Gospel groups of their time – their influence led to Pops' friendship with Martin Luther King and involvement in the Civil Rights' movement. Pops is still making fine records, while daughter Mavis now spends much of her time playing and recording with Prince – or Squiggle, as we should now call him. Recommended: 'Respect Yourself' (Ace/Stax 006); 'Father Father' (Virgin PointBlank CD19)

Robert Stroger

(Born 27 December 1930 Haiti Missouri)
Now one of the best-known bassists in Chicago, Bob Stroger moved to the city in the late Forties. Stroger dabbled in Jazz ('and nearly starved to death!') and played with a wide variety of local musicians until joining up with Otis Rush in the early Seventies in a musical relationship that lasted nearly a decade. Since then Stroger has played regularly with Sunnyland Slim, Jimmy Rogers, and Mississippi Heat.

Hubert Sumlin

(Born 16 November 1931, Greenwood Miss)
From the time he joined Howlin' Wolf's band in 1954, Hubert Sumlin played an integral part in countless classic songs such as 'Spoonful', 'Evil' and 'Killing Floor'. Sumlin's style is unique: edgy and unpredictable, employing a kind of lateral guitar thinking that makes him impossible to imitate. Apart from his work with Wolf, Sumlin also toured and recorded with Muddy Waters and played guitar on several Chuck Berry hits. Sadly, though, his abundant skills have never been truly captured on a solo recording. Hopefully a recording project with Taj Mahal in 1995 will rectify matters. Recommended (with Howlin' Wolf): 'Spoonful' (Charly CDRB2); 'The Chess Box' (MCA/Chess CHD3-9332)

Sunnyland Slim

(Born 5 September 1907, Vance Miss)
Sunnyland Slim, born Albert Luandrew, was one of the supreme operators of the Blues, who helped encourage the Chess brothers move into the Blues field and gave countless musicians, including Muddy Waters and Little Walter, their first break. Sunnyland was also a shrewd hustler, who often made more money via his various lucrative sidelines than through music.
Luandrew left home while in his early teens, as a result of his father's remarriage, and played piano in juke joints and at a movie theatre before moving to Memphis in 1925, where he was given the Sunnyland name after his signature song, Sunnyland Train. Sunnyland worked with many Delta musicians in Memphis, but when the mayor closed down many of the city's gambling joints and brothels, cruelly curtailing his income, Sunnyland moved over to West Memphis and opened up his own gambling joint. By 1942 Sunnyland had moved to Chicago, where he would become one of the city's leading band leaders; he would work with many local stalwarts including Tampa Red, Doctor Clayton, Muddy Waters, Robert Lockwood Jr, and JB Lenoir, and recorded for many labels both under his own name, and backing other artists. As a pianist, Sunnyland was somewhat overlooked when electric Blues became regarded as a guitar-led medium, but there was never any doubt in the city about Sunnyland's pre-eminence. A deeply religious man, despite or

perhaps because of his eventful past, Sunnyland was still fixing up his basement as his own private club when he died in 1995. Recommended: 'Sunnyland Slim' (Flyright 566); 'Be Careful How You Vote' (Earwig 4915).

Koko Taylor
(Born 28 September 1935, Memphis Tenn)
Taylor, born Cora Walton, sang Gospel songs at church, but developed a taste for Blues listening to the Memphis-based WDIA radio station. When husband Pops Taylor decided to move to Chicago in 1953, Koko insisted on accompanying him and was soon guesting at Chicago clubs before being talent-spotted by Willie Dixon, who produced 1965's 'Wang Dang Doodle'. 'Wang Dang Doodle' was Chess' last real chart success in the Blues field, and as the label's sales suffered in the late Sixties, so did Taylor. However, a move to Bruce Iglauer's newly-established Alligator Records in 1974 prompted a resurgence in her career which continues to this day. Recommended: ' What It Takes/The Chess Years' (MCA/Chess 9328); 'Queen Of The Blues' (Alligator 4740)

Tabby Thomas
(Born 5 January 1929, Baton Rouge La)
Best known for his Blues Box club in Baton Rouge, Tabby Thomas started out as a Blues crooner in the Charles Brown style. Thomas's best-known records were made at Jay Miller's recording studio in Crawley Louisiana, including 1962's 'Hoodoo Party', which was released on the Excello label and features on several Excello compilations including 'Excello Authentic R&B' (Ace CDCHD492) Thomas has also released records on his own Blue Beat label.

Henry Townsend
(Born October 27, 1909, Shelby Miss)
Henry Townsend has been one of the leading figures in the St Louis music scene since the late Twenties. Originally a guitarist, Townsend switched to piano under the influence of Roosevelt Sykes; he worked with such luminaries as Robert Nighthawk, Robert Johnson and Sonny Boy Williamson II and recorded for the Columbia, Paramount and Bluebird labels during the Thirties, before, as he puts it, the first Blues boom turned to bust.

Othar Turner
(Born 2 June 1907, Jackson Miss)
Marshall County Mississippi has always exhibited musical traditions which are quite distinct from the rest of the state, most notably the fife and drum music which some musicologists maintain is in direct descent from African traditions. Turner is one of the area's leading fife players, and still regularly plays Blues festivals and local picnics with a band led by daughter Bernice.

Jimmie Vaughan
(Born 20 March 1951, Dallas Tx)
Jimmie Vaughan was a prime mover in the development of the Austin Blues scene that grew up around Antone's club in the Seventies. Vaughan was famous both for the no-frills guitar style he established with The Fabulous Thunderbirds, and for inspiring his more extrovert younger brother Stevie Ray, who would become the major trailblazer for the Blues in the Eighties. It was in fact the younger sibling who broke first, with 1983's 'Texas Flood' album – the Thunderbirds would have to wait until 1986 for their first hit, 'Tuff Enuff'. In 1990 the brothers collaborated for the first time on the celebrated 'Family Style', a good-time romp through Blues, Country and Soul territories that was horribly overshadowed by Stevie's death in a helicopter crash in 1990. Jimmie Vaughan subsequently spent considerable time assembling Steve's remaining recordings before returning with 1994's 'Strange Pleasure', which shows him to be one of the most versatile and concise guitar stylists of the Nineties.
Recommended: (as The Vaughan Brothers) 'Family Style' (Epic 4670142); Strange Pleasure (Epic 4670142)

Johnny Vincent
(Born 25 April 1925 Laurel Miss)
Vincent was a talent spotter for Art Rupe's Specialty label, signing such luminaries as Guitar Slim before branching out with his own label, Ace (no connection with the UK label of the same name). Ace scored many hits with the likes of Earl King and Huey Smith before moving into white-oriented music, but despite scoring hits such as Jimmy Clanton's 'Venus In Blue Jeans', an ill-starred deal with Vee Jay records forced the company into liquidation. Vincent has recently re-launched Ace, and is intending to sign new acts as well as exploiting his back catalogue.

Jimmie Walker
(Born 8 March 1905, Memphis Tenn)
One of the most senior figures on the Chicago Blues scene, pianist Jimmie Walker arrived to the city around 1908, and learned the piano while in his early teens. By the Twenties Walker was regularly playing local clubs and house parties with Lonnie Johnson and Homesick James, but after a decade in the Chicago clubs he moved out of the music business. Cousin Homesick James was partly responsible for Walker's return to the business in the mid Fifties, when Walker played with Elmore James, Billy Boy Arnold and others, while a partnership with fellow Chicago pianist Erwin Helfer resulted in his belated debut recording in 1964. Walker still plays piano and is a regular attraction at the Northside Chicago club Blues on Halsted.

Joe Louis Walker
(Born 25 December 1949, San Francisco Ca)
Walker grew up listening to his parents' Blues records, and by the mid Sixties was perfectly placed to enjoy the West Coast Blues Boom, backing up the likes of Earl Hooker and Lightnin' Hopkins at San Francisco clubs. By the Seventies, however, Walker was disillusioned with the Rock business and took a decade-long break to sing Gospel. In 1986 Walker made a widely-publicised return to the Blues genre with 'Cold Is The Night', which helped establish him as one of the most popular of a new generation of Bluesmen - and possibly the last generation to learn their craft directly from the original masters. Recommended: 'Cold Is The Night' (Ace CDCHM208)

Robert Ward
(Born 15 October 1938, Luthersville Ga)
For many years, Ward was known as the man who contributed the haunting guitar lines to 'I Found A Love', a 1962 hit by the Falcons, with one Wilson Pickett on vocals. Later on Ward formed the Ohio Untouchables, who would evolve into million-selling funksters The Ohio Players. It was really only Ward's rediscovery by Hammond Scott of the Black Top label that showed what a talent he is – a superb guitarist (listen to Robert Cray's later CDs to hear the influence of his intricate 'Magnatone' vibrato'd rhythm/lead style), a skilled Soul songwriter, and no slouch on the vocal front either. On form, his live performances put his admittedly impressive records to shame.
Recommended: 'Fear No Evil' (Blacktop/Silvertone 520); 'Rhythm Of The People' (Black Top 1088)

Johnny Guitar Watson
(Born 3 February 1935, Houston Tx)
Starting out as another Texas guitarist in the Guitar Slim/ Gatemouth Brown mould, Johnny Guitar Watson soon showed more than a hint of welcome individuality. There were gimmicky songs such as 'Space Guitar', witty wordplay on material such as 'Gangster Of Love', later covered by Steve Miller, but his greatest moments are probably those dismissed by Blues fundamentalists, when he turned to funk in the Seventies and came up with a string of masterful and witty albums on DJM: 'Ain't That A Bitch', 'A Real Mother For Ya', and 'Funk Beyond The Call Of Duty'. Watson is a brilliant instrumentalist – Frank Zappa was a fervent fan of his guitar playing – while, let's face it, if he were white he would be rated alongside Bob Dylan or Elvis Costello as a lyricist supreme. Recommended: 'Three Hours Past Midnight' (Ace CDCH909); 'Gangster Of Love' (Charly CD267). Watson's DJM albums are in the process of being re-released.

Jr Wells
(Born 9 December 1934, Memphis Tenn)
Jr Wells first achieved fame in Chicago when he replaced Little Walter in Muddy Waters' band; he later went on to form one of the most electrifying Blues partnerships of the Sixties with Buddy Guy.
Amos 'Jr' Wells played occasionally with Sunnyland Slim and Robert Lockwood in his youth, before moving to Chicago and teaming up with Dave and Louis Myers as the Three Aces. With Jazzer Fred Below persuaded to join on drums, the all-electric Aces became one of the city's hippest acts, before Wells swapped places with Little Walter and joined the Waters band. Wells stayed with Waters, off and on, for the next three years, then briefly reformed the Aces, before teaming up with Buddy Guy in 1958. They were a potent partnership, eclectic and extrovert, who occasionally succeeded in making ex-employers such as Muddy Waters look tired and perfunctory. Wells embodied Chicago street chic, always immaculately dressed in suits with creases so sharp they could have been crafted from sheet steel, and though his career suffered when Guy scored a solo deal in the early Nineties, Wells is still, on a good night, electrifying. Recommended: 'Messing With The Kid' (Charly 219); 'Hoodoo Man Blues' (Delmark 612)